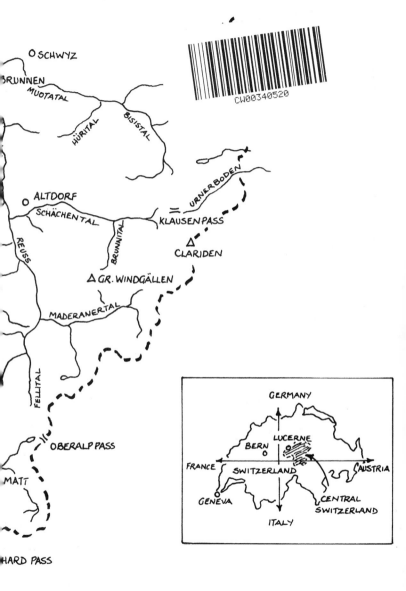

CENTRAL SWITZERLAND

At Nideralp above the Schächental (Route 42)

CENTRAL SWITZERLAND

A Walking Guide

by

KEV REYNOLDS

CICERONE PRESS
MILNTHORPE, CUMBRIA

© Kev Reynolds 1993
ISBN 1 85284 131 1

A catalogue record for this book is available from the British Library

ACKNOWLEDGEMENTS

I am grateful, as ever, to Heidi Reisz at the Swiss National Tourist Office in London for generous assistance during research for this guidebook. The staff of many other tourist offices in the Central Switzerland region were also very helpful, and in particular I wish to acknowledge the kindness shown by Mayer Vogler in Sarnen, Ruedi Willi in Brunnen and Brigitte Bucher in Lucerne. My publishers are thanked for their continued encouragement and for supplying me with the best excuse of all to spend my summers wandering in the mountains. Sharing some of the most memorable days were my daughter Ilsa and friend Jill Crocker and, of course, my wife Linda whose love and practical support, especially in keeping the home together while I remain behind to finish research among the Alps, is the best gift of all. To them all I offer my thanks.

Kev Reynolds

Cicerone Press guidebooks by the same author:
Walks in the Engadine - Switzerland
The Valais - Switzerland
The Jura *(with R Brian Evans)*
The Bernese Alps
Ticino - Switzerland
Alpine Pass Route
Chamonix to Zermatt - the Walker's Haute Route
Walks & Climbs in the Pyrenees
The Wealdway & The Vanguard Way
The South Downs Way & The Downs Link
The Cotswold Way
Walking in Kent
Annapurna

Front Cover: Titlis dominates the view from Dagenstal above Engelberg.
(Routes 81, 82, 83)

CONTENTS

INTRODUCTION 7
    MOUNTAINS OF CENTRAL SWITZERLAND 12
    HOW TO GET THERE 14
    TRANSPORT WITHIN THE REGION 15
    ACCOMMODATION 17
    MOUNTAIN FLOWERS 21
    MOUNTAIN ANIMALS 23
    WEATHER 25
    NOTES FOR WALKERS 26
    PATHS AND WAYMARKS 29
    SAFETY IN THE MOUNTAINS 30
    GRADING OF WALKS 32
    RECOMMENDED MAPS 33
    USING THE GUIDE 33

VIERWALDSTÄTTERSEE (LAKE OF LUCERNE)
    Lucerne, Weggis, Vitznau, Brunnen, Sisikon, Flüelen, Altdorf,
    Seelisberg 35
MUOTATAL
    Schwyz, Muotathal 78
KLAUSENPASS REGION
    Altdorf, Burglen, Unterschächen, Urnerboden 102
MADERANERTAL
    Amsteg, Bristen, Golzern 126
UPPER URI
    Andermatt, Hospental, Realp 136

GÖSCHENER TAL
  Göschenen 151
MEIENTAL
  Wassen 164
MELCHTAL AND SARNER AA
  Lungern, Sarnen, Kerns, Melchtal, Melchsee-Frutt 171
ENGELBERGERTAL
  Engelberg 183

APPENDIX A: Useful Addresses 202
APPENDIX B: Glossary 203
BIBLIOGRAPHY 204
ROUTE INDEX 205

INTRODUCTION

At the heart of Central Switzerland lies the Vierwaldstättersee, the Lake of the Four Forest Cantons - better known to English-speaking visitors as the Lake of Lucerne.

Not only does it form the heart of the region covered by this guidebook, it also lays claim, with some justification, to be the very heart of Switzerland itself, for it was on the banks of the Urnersee (the southern projecting finger of the lake) that the Swiss Confederation was born 700 years ago. The Rütli Meadow on the western shore, said to be the meeting place of the founding fathers of the Confederation, is virtually a place of pilgrimage, a green tilted site of unspoilt simplicity that has come to represent the Swiss spirit of independence, hard-won and jealously guarded.

From Rütli Meadow you gaze over a landscape of lake, forest, pasture and mountain. On the far side of the Urnersee villages dot the shoreline. Above them steep sloping alps are punctuated with chalets, haybarns and tiny hamlets. Wisps of cloud dust summit snows on mountains sliced here and there with valleys that tease; valleys in whose secret depths wind trails that help unravel the peace and splendour of this alpine heartland.

Irregular in shape, the Lake of Lucerne must be one of the most beautiful in all of Europe. Rising from its shores two particular mountains that have been known and loved for centuries reveal panoramas of unparalleled magnificence from their easily-accessible summits. The first is Pilatus which overlooks Lucerne itself. Immediately below lakes and soft pasturelands spread patterns of tranquillity, but off to the south stretches a long wall of snowpeaks, several of whose shapely individual summits are recognisable from afar; the chain of the Bernese Alps. Well to the east of Lucerne rises the Rigi, a long sloping wedge of mountain that forms a rough block between the Vierwaldstättersee and the Zugersee. This too gazes south to a lovely wall of mountains, but these are mountains of the Central Swiss Alps; not nearly so well-known as those of the Bernese Alps, perhaps, but certainly no less remarkable, no less scenically spectacular.

From Pilatus and from Rigi the rich diversity of Central Switzerland is laid out for inspection. There is something here for everyone who delights in scenic splendour: neat tended pastures, gentle lakeside paths, easy summits, raw crags, glaciers and snowfields, mountain-locked tarns, huge waterfalls, limestone pavements, trout-filled rivers, deep gorges, open flower-starred plateaux...There are attractive villages, culture-rich towns, historic sites. There are cableways, rack railways and lake steamers that reveal aspects of beauty without the effort of walking. There are challenging walks, opportunities for lazy lake-side days, hidden glens lost to all but the most adventurous of wanderers, high passes to cross, marmot, chamois and deer to stalk, long views to dream on...

Something, indeed, for everyone.

Geographically Central Switzerland is a complex region covering several cantons, but if we imagine it as a wheel, with Lucerne as its hub, much of the country to the south and east of the lake is that which is included in this guide. It's a region in which the mountains and valleys are so many spokes in the wheel, with other spokes, or valleys, cutting away from them swastika-like into assorted mountain massifs.

Begin by heading clockwise from Lucerne. East of the Vierwaldstättersee the Rigi is the dominant mountain mass with the lakeside resorts of Weggis and Vitznau providing mechanized access to its upper slopes. To the north and east lie other lakes: Zugersee in the north, bordered by low green hills, and the smaller Lauerzersee from whose soft shores views are either to the Rigi or to the twin Mythen peaks that rise above Schwyz, a small town whose name was adopted and adapted to encompass the whole country.

Schwyz sits at a junction of roads, one of which snakes eastward to the Muotatal offering superb walking possibilities by way of the Pragel Pass, Bisistal and Hurital. From each of these tributary valleys streams flow down to join the Muota, whose alluvial deposits have formed a low-lying strand on which Brunnen sits facing across the narrow lake channel where the Urnersee projects fjord-like from the main body of the Vierwaldstättersee.

The eastern wall of the Urnersee is uncompromisingly steep, yet there are walks to be had along midheight shelves of pastureland with superb views across the lake, or down to the broad trench of the Reuss valley that narrows in the south as it climbs and is squeezed by a mass of lofty mountains. Flüelen squats near the end of the lake. Altdorf is its better-known neighbour a short distance away at the foot of the Schächental where a serpentine road writhes up to the Klausenpass. Both sides of the Klausenpass offer grand country to discover on foot. On the eastern side lies Urnerboden, a beautiful, broad, U-shaped valley walled by Dolomite-like cliffs to the north and by the snow and ice of Clariden and Gemsfairenstock to the south. To the west of the pass the Schächental boasts one of Switzerland's finest waterfalls spraying from its head above the tiny village of Äsch. On both sides of the valley there are high belvedere trails. There are foot passes to cross on the northern side which lead into the Muotatal, while cutting south of Unterschächen another splendid tributary glen, the Brunnital, heads towards the Windgällen massif.

Windgällen itself is more often approached from the peaceful, back-country valley of the Maderanertal which drains into the narrows of the Reuss gorge at Amsteg, while the western side of the Reuss valley holds a tight cluster of peaks - and more challenging country for mountain walkers - between Altdorf and Engelberg. But before we look at that delightful corner, mention should be made of the Fellital, an amazing valley, quite uninhabited save for a few remote alp huts where goats' cheese is made in summer; a glen of unsophisticated magic with an easy walker's pass at its head that leads to the Oberalp Pass.

Andermatt lies at the confluence of major trans-alpine routes. The Oberalp Pass, by which the valley of the Vorder-Rhein is gained, rises above to the east. To the west of the town is the Furka Pass, which either descends on its far side through Goms to the valley of the Rhone dividing the southern Bernese Alps and the Pennine Alps of canton Valais, or gives access to the Grimsel, heading north by way of the Haslital to the mainstream resorts of the Bernese Oberland. But south of Andermatt is the Gotthard, one of the most important of pass routes linking northern Europe with Mediterranean Italy. Historically significant, it is a major transit route today with road and rail tunnels disappearing into the mountains that wall Ticino.

Downstream a short distance to the north of Andermatt stands Göschenen, with its own secretive valley probing westward. Head into the Göschener Tal and you come to an alpine wonderland. At the head of the main Göschener Tal there's an unsung tributary glen, the Voralp, worth exploring a few short kilometres inside the valley. There's a large dammed lake, and above that the ramparts of the Winterberg, whose highest summit is the Dammastock (3630m), topped with snow and draped with glaciers. Another inner glen, the Chelenalptal, is accessible from the end of the lake. Glaciers tail down into it from the Hinter Tierberg, but where these icefields have withdrawn alpenroses are now taking over and colour blazes among the ageing moraines. It's all so uncouth yet magnificent; country to wander into with heart singing.

North again from Göschenen another major valley cuts back north-westward from the main valley of the Reuss. This is the Meiental through which traffic grinds on the way to the Susten Pass. Yet away from the road this too gives plenty of scope for walking, while the peaks that block the valley are as spiritually uplifting as any.

The irregular block of mountains between the Furka and Susten consists of big glaciated peaks with a challenging heartland, in effect an extension of the eastern Bernese Alps. But to the north of the Susten is another, larger area crossed by no roads at all between that of the Reuss on the eastern side and the Lucerne-Brünig Pass road on the west. The Vierwaldstättersee forms a natural boundary to the north, and there are only three routes of access that cut into these mountains - two from the north and one from the south. The two northerly access routes are those that lead to Engelberg, virtually in the centre of this large block, and the narrow seasonal road to Melchsee-Frutt. That which provides entry to motorists from the south is the quiet road leading from the Gadmental into the Gental with the gleaming tarn of Engstlensee a short distance from the road-head. Although road access is severely limited in this large mountainous area, the walker comes into his own here. It is very much a walker's paradise, a land of great beauty and many contrasts.

The final spoke in our imaginary wheel is created by the valley of the Sarner Aa which drains north of the Brünig Pass and enters the Vierwaldstättersee by way of the Alpnachersee at the foot of Pilatus. It is from this valley that one gains access to the high pastures of the Melchtal and Melchsee-Frutt, but the valley itself has much to commend it without straying far. There are three lakes, green and pleasant meadowlands, patches of forest and enticing views south to the distant Wetterhorn which, of course, overlooks Grindelwald in the neighbouring Bernese Alps.

So, Central Switzerland may be geographically complicated, but it offers a magnificent choice of terrain for a walking holiday. Those who enjoy soft, seductive valleys in which to amble, who are happy to take advantage of mechanisation to gain high viewpoints and then to wander down, will find themselves spoilt for choice in the hills on either side of the northern Vierwaldstättersee, while those who prefer a more rugged landscape will be well content with the wild country accessed from the Göschener Tal in the south. In between there's a middle course, and plenty of it too: a middle course of green but challenging hillsides; valleys full of alpine charm, with belvedere trails that link isolated summer-only hamlets; valleys with no proper road into them, just a dirt track used by farmers or maybe a mule-trail that has yet to bear the imprint of a motor vehicle's wheel.

Here in the very heart of Switzerland, just a short distance from some of Europe's major transit routes, a modest few kilometres from tourist-thronged resorts, it is possible to wander for days at a time even in mid-summer and see but a tiny handful of people. In this respect Central Switzerland is something of a conundrum. This guidebook offers an opportunity to explore some of the very best it has to offer. None who love mountain scenery on a grand scale need ever be disappointed.

MOUNTAINS OF CENTRAL SWITZERLAND

None of the modest peaks of the Central Swiss Alps can compete for familiarity with many of those that crowd the Pennine or Bernese Alps, yet height, fame or notoriety are no yardsticks of beauty and numerous mountains here stand proud in comparative anonymity - either in clustered groups or in isolated splendour.

Mention has already been made of the long northern wall of the Urnerboden valley east of the Klausenpass. This wall, running from the Läckistock, over the jagged Jegerstock to the Ortstock, barely tops 2600 metres, but it has an unquestionable beauty of almost Dolomite-like rawness. Enter the valley from the east and the eye is drawn along this continuous shaft of soaring grey stone. Climb up onto its mid-height balcony above Urnerboden village and a close acquaintance reveals bold individual towers like a series of organ pipes set in a row.

Opposite rises Clariden (3268m) with its small drape of glacier hanging in the upper north-facing corrie, while its south-east and south-western flanks are a broad sweep of snow and ice surrounded by satellite peaklets. A near neighbour to the south-east is the Tödi (3614m), sometimes known as the King of the Little Mountains. This too has a modest glacial adornment that drains into the Linthal. Tödi and its neighbours, on the borders of cantons Glarus and Graubunden, were among the earliest of alpine groups to be explored, for many of the summits were climbed in the late eighteenth and early nineteenth centuries by Father Placidus à Spescha, a monk who, at various times, served in the abbeys at Disentis and Einsiedeln, and at the hospice on the Lukmanier Pass. In 1824, at the age of seventy-two, he made an attempt to climb the Tödi with two chamois hunters. Too tired to continue beyond what is today known as the Porta de Spescha, he was nonetheless content to see his companions reach the summit for the first time.

The southern flanks of the Tödi group fall to the valley of the Vorder-Rhein, but the southern snowfields and glaciers of nearby Clariden are boosted by others from the Chammliberg and Schärhorn to sweep down as the Hüfifirn into the head of the lovely Maderanertal.

Chli (or Klein) Ruchen (2944m) and Gross Dussi (3256m) form gateposts to the lower Hüfifirn, the latter an attractive peak, especially when viewed from the Windgällen hut on the western side of the valley. The Windgällen is a rocky collection of spires and turrets, virtually ice-free, but crusted with screes.

The north wall of the Gross Windgällen is linked with that of the Gross Ruchen and Chli Ruchen which plunge steeply into the head of the little Brunnital and effectively create a superb amphitheatre that is best seen from the depths of the Brunnital itself. Entered from Unterschächen this is one of the most enchanting glens in the whole region.

West of the Reuss valley, opposite the Maderanertal, the outliers of the Titlis group are best represented by the Spannort pinnacles (Gross Spannort 3198m; Klein Spannort 3140m). Walkers exploring the Surenen valley above Engelberg are treated to a teasing glimpse of their upper crags, but when seen from the high path through the Abnet pastures they appear to have been transported en mass from the Dolomites and make a dramatic contrast to the great square-cut block of the nearby Titlis (3238m).

Titlis boasts huge walls, particularly on its eastern and southern sides, while cupped on the upper north and west-facing flanks is a vast tilted slope of ice and snow - a paradise for skiers. First climbed by monks in 1739 the mountain is today laced with numerous mechanical aids, with one leading right to the summit of the Klein Titlis (3028m). With such temptation at hand it has become an extremely popular mountain with visitors both winter and summer. From its summit a fine panorama of snowpeaks encompasses not only neighbours of the Central Swiss Alps, but also many giants of the Bernese Alps too.

Rising from the Göschener Tal mention must be made of the Salbitschijen (2981m) whose ridges form the eastern wall of the lower Voralp. As a challenge for rock climbers the Salbitschijen has much of appeal; its magnificent South Ridge first attracted, then was won, by Otto Amstad and Guido Masetto in 1935.

Towards the head of the Voralp valley, and seen to good effect from the Voralp hut, the Sustenhorn (3503m) shows a series of steep cliffs rising dramatically from a turmoil of glaciers, but the largest icefields of the district are to be found hanging on the eastern flanks of the Winterberg above the dammed lake of the Göscheneralpsee. The Dammastock (3630m) dominates the Winterberg wall from its central position. But it is the full unrestrained sweep of rock and ice of the lengthy Winterberg itself which creates such an impression of impregnability. As you approach through the morainic wilderness of the Dammareuss glen, sliced by the dashing glacial torrent, you can almost sense a primeval mood of untamed majesty. Such impressions are similarly gained on the approach to the Chelenalp hut high above the Chelenalptal to the north. The Chelen glacier that carved this valley has withdrawn considerably and is now seen as a tail of ice dangling below the Tierberg group where the complicated Hinter Tierberg has a number of summits, highest of which tops 3447 metres. The Chelenalp hut is perched high above the valley floor, and from it the walker enjoys a grand dress circle view of a rough cirque of rock and ice which encloses the upper valley in a savage horseshoe.

HOW TO GET THERE

Travel to Switzerland is direct and without complication, whether one journeys by road, rail or air. International airports are situated at Basle, Bern, Geneva and Zürich, and regular scheduled flights between the U.K. and Switzerland are operated out of London (Heathrow and Gatwick) by Swissair and British Airways to Geneva, Basle and Zürich and with additional flights from Manchester, Birmingham and Dublin. Full information regarding flights may be obtained from the Swiss National Tourist Office whose address is given in the Appendix.

From North America air services fly to Geneva and/or Zürich from Boston, Chicago, Los Angeles, Montreal and New York. Swissair is just one airline that maintains a trans-Atlantic service.

Each of the main airports within Switzerland is served with reliable train or bus services to town terminals. Zürich or Bern are the most convenient airports for visitors to Central Switzerland, and a rail link from both towns provides speedy access to Lucerne. The trans-alpine Gotthard line traverses the region from north to south, thus providing an additional fast rail link.

If travelling by rail from the U.K. the most obvious route to take would be London (Victoria) to Calais, Basle, Zürich and Lucerne, Flüelen, Göschenen or Andermatt. Local trains and/or Postbus connections will continue the journey from major stations with admirable efficiency.

For those already in the Alps the Furka Oberalp Bahn and the Glacier Express, both of which touch the southern part of the region, stop at Andermatt and could prove useful.

By road a first-class network of motorways (*Autobahn*) criss-cross Switzerland to enable a fast journey to be made to the region covered by this book. From Basle the N2 goes to Lucerne and round the southern shore of the Vierwaldstättersee to Altdorf, then through the Reuss valley to Andermatt en route to the Gotthard tunnel. From Zürich the N4 goes round the northern end of the Zugersee and forks near Rotkreuz. The N14 breaks away to Lucerne, while the continuing N4 keeps to the west of the Zugersee and goes via Schwyz along the Axenstrasse to join the N2 near Altdorf.

Note that all vehicles using the motorway system in Switzerland need a special *vignette* - proof of payment of a motorway tax. This *vignette* may be purchased in advance from the Swiss National Tourist Office, or alternatively at the point of entry into the country.

TRANSPORT WITHIN THE REGION

The Swiss public transport system is legendary. It is a highly efficient network; punctual, comprehensive and, for the walker with or without his own vehicle, of inestimable value. From a single valley base you can travel to any one of a number of locations by Postbus, train or lake paddle steamer to begin a day's walk. And when a walk begins from your base and aims in a single direction along the valley or across a pass into a neighbouring district, there will often be a convenient means of returning to the hotel or campsite at the end of the day.

Railways serve much of the country covered by this book. Lucerne, of course, has a major station, but at the other end of the region Andermatt is also an important junction. In between, several minor towns and villages along the Reuss valley also have stations that could be very useful to walkers. Trains from Lucerne serve Engelberg. Another line travels by way of Sarnen and Giswil to cross the Brunig Pass into the Bernese Alps. Trains run from Lucerne to Küssnacht and Brunnen, and along the eastern bank of the Vierwaldstättersee to Flüelen.

Yellow Postbuses serve those areas where there are no railways. As the name implies they are operated by the postal service and are as predictably punctual as are the railways, being a symbol of Swiss efficiency. The region covered by this guide is admirably served, with practically every village having a bus route to it - if not a Postbus, then a vehicle owned by a private company licensed by the postal service. Of particular value is the route over the Klausenpass between Altdorf and Linthal. So too are the following routes: round the southern side of the Vierwaldstättersee between Stans and Altdorf; between Sarnen and Melchsee-Frutt and from Göschenen to the dammed lake in the Göschener Tal.

In village centres the main Postbus pick-up will be outside the local post office (PTT). In outlying areas railway stations will also have a PTT bus stop, and there are certain strategic points without habitation in some valleys where passengers may be picked up on request. Look for the PTT *Haltestelle* sign. Other than at these specific points, passengers should buy their tickets in advance at the post office. By pre-purchasing tickets this way the driver will be able to maintain his schedule.

Another useful form of public transport in the region is lake steamer on the Vierwaldstättersee which provides a romantic start or finish to a day's walking. It can be an effective option, especially for those planning to tackle the Swiss Path, to take one example. The Lake Lucerne Navigation Company operates no less than twenty-one boats, five of them paddle steamers, and one departure leaves Lucerne approximately every hour through the summer. Such lakeside resorts as Brunnen and Flüelen are served with appreciable frequency and there are numerous calling points on all shores of the lake.

In addition to the network of rail, boat and Postbus services, various cableways and cog railways exist throughout Central Switzerland which the walker can use to great advantage. Where these occur, mention is made in the text.

A number of incentives are available to holiday makers planning to make use of rail, bus or lake steamer in Switzerland. The Swiss Pass is one. Valid for periods of three, eight or fifteen days, or for one month, the Pass allows unlimited travel throughout the country by almost every train, boat or Postbus route, as well as discounts on a number of cableways. With a special Family Reduction Card, children under fifteen can take advantage of free travel if accompanied by parents holding a Swiss Pass. Enquire for full details at the Swiss National Tourist Office.

A Regional Pass, covering much of the area included in this book (but nothing south or east of Altdorf), is valid for a period of either seven or fifteen days, during which unlimited travel is allowed on certain days on set routes, and on the remaining days all travel is available at half fare. This Pass is useful for trips by boat, rail, bus and cableway, and may be purchased at tourist offices, railway stations and boat ticket offices.

A Family Card is also available, free of charge, from railway stations. This allows free travel on trains for children up to sixteen years, and half-fare for those between 16 and 25, as long as both parents pay standard fare. Again, full details are available from the Swiss National Tourist Office.

ACCOMMODATION

Accommodation of all kinds should be found right across the region. The Swiss, of course, have a long tradition of hotel-keeping, and with so many resorts large and small liberally scattered throughout Central Switzerland, there will be plenty of every standard of lodging to meet the requirements of holiday makers no matter what their financial resources might be. Whilst Switzerland in general has the reputation of being somewhat expensive, it is quite possible to enjoy a very fine walking holiday there without it costing a small fortune. There are several campsites, youth hostels and moderately-priced inns and *pensions*. There are various *Matratzenlagers* (inns with dormitory-style accommodation) that would suit the pockets of those who are content with spartan sociability, and there are extremely grand hotels for those without wallet restrictions. There are also, of course, hundreds of intermediate hotels and *Gasthofs* and, in a number of resorts, a growing list of chalets or apartments available for short-term rent.

And there are mountain huts that have an undeniable appeal all their own.

For valley-based accommodation the tourist information office in practically every small town or village will be able to supply a list giving the full range available, from the cheapest to the most expensive. Swiss National Tourist Offices should also be able to provide information. SNTO offices normally stock the *Swiss Hotel Guide* published annually by the Swiss Hotel Association which lists addresses, rates and amenities of some 2500 hotels and pensions throughout the country. A smaller edition is published which covers detail of just those hotels and *pensions* within Central Switzerland. Ask for the *Central Switzerland Hotel Guide*.

Camping: Official campsites exist in several of the region's valleys. One or two of these offer rather basic facilities, while others not only have first-class toilet and washing blocks, but also provide laundry and drying rooms. Engelberg's campsite even boasts an indoor swimming pool and sauna! However, one should not automatically assume that because campers are provided for in one of the larger, better-known resorts its facilities will reflect the affluence of the area. The converse is often true. By contrast, some of the smaller villages take a pride in the provision of their campsites, and the holiday maker will appreciate the standards on offer. Mention is made within this book where campsites exist, but in general comments are limited with regard to facilities provided, since they may change from year to year.

Off-site camping is officially discouraged throughout the country.

Bearing in mind the limited amount of land available for pasture or hay-making, this is perhaps understandable. Uncontrolled camping could inflict considerable damage to a peasant farmer's short season crop of meadowland hay. Above the tree-line, though, the considerate backpacker may find a suitably remote corner far from any alp which could accommodate a small tent for a short overnight stay. In such cases the practice may go unnoticed or without comment. Should you choose to take advantage of such a wilderness camp, please be discreet, be prudent in your actions, take great care not to foul water sources and be scrupulous with regard to carrying away all rubbish when you move on.

Youth Hostels: Several youth hostels belonging to the SJH *(Schweizerischer Bund für Jugendherbergen)* are located in the area covered by this guidebook. Anyone holding a current membership card of the Hostels Association of his own country can use hostels in Switzerland, but priority is given to members below the age of twenty-five. Visitors wishing to take advantage of hostels in Central Switzerland are advised to join their home organisation before setting out. Emergency international membership is possible to arrange at Swiss hostels, but will be far more expensive than joining at home.

Dormitory accommodation is offered in all youth hostels. In some, smaller twin-bedded rooms may be available, but these should not be expected. Meals may be provided at some, but not in all of them, and those regular hostel-users in the U.K. will be disappointed to discover that self-catering facilities are not of the same standard as on offer at most YHA or SYHA hostels.

Matratzenlagers: Similar to the *gîtes d'étape* of France, *Matratzenlagers* offer basic dormitory accommodation for travellers and are located in assorted buildings - on farms, in the attic of rustic mountain inns or even in the annexe of a standard-grade hotel. Facilities on offer vary enormously. I have experienced superb self-catering kitchens and unlimited access to hot showers in some, and inn meals and a trough of cold running water in others. Prices are generally much lower than those charged in hotels and gasthofs, and are more or less in line with youth hostels, but without the necessity for membership of an organisation. There are a number of *Matratzenlagers* within Central Switzerland, but they are not publicised to any degree. If interested ask specifically at the local tourist information office for details of any in the vicinity.

Mountain Huts: A number of walks described within these pages visit mountain huts belonging to club sections affiliated to the SAC *(Schweizer Alpen Club)*. Some require a long approach and an overnight is advised.

Walkers familiar with the mountain hut system in the Alps will require no advice from me and need read no farther, but first-time users might find a few words helpful. Firstly, mountain huts *(Hütte, refuge* or *cabane)* vary considerably in their standards of accommodation and degree of comfort, if not in basic facilities provided. In recent years many SAC huts have been quite substantially renovated, improved and enlarged in response to increased demands, and those prospective hut users who have only read of somewhat primitive conditions experienced in the past will be surprised by some of these improvements. It should be stressed, however, that such improvements are not evident in all huts.

Sleeping quarters are invariably of the dormitory variety: in most cases upon a large communal platform with a plentiful supply of mattresses, blankets and pillows, but no sheets. There is no segregation of the sexes. If the hut is busy, and most will be in the height of the summer season, this type of sleeping arrangement can very soon lose any attraction it might otherwise be deemed to hold. In huts used by climbers quiet is expected to be observed by about 9.00pm, but be prepared to be rudely waken as early as 2.00am as they rise to set out on their chosen route!

On arrival at the hut and finding sufficient room, it is best to lay claim to your bedspace whilst there is light to do so. Boots should not be worn inside the hut, but left on a rack situated near the entrance. A supply of hut shoes is usually provided.

Most huts have a guardian who will allocate bedspace and often provide meals. These will usually be substantial in quantity, although they are not exactly noted for being gourmet cuisine. Plentiful quantities of tea and soup are usually available, and there will normally be bottled drinks for sale. In some cases, depending upon situation, there will be no natural supply of drinking water, in which case the guardian will sell boiled or treated water by the litre. Water at the washroom tap is seldom drinkable.

Most unguarded huts have self-cooking facilities available and all the visitor need provide is food. Cooking equipment, crockery and cutlery should be found in the hut. If you plan to use an unguarded hut, please make every effort to leave it in a clean and tidy condition.

Overnight fees are not cheap. Remote buildings are expensive to build and maintain, and the cost of supplying them with food and equipment is aggravated by the distance everything has to be carried from the valley. Formerly supplied by mule or by porter, these days foodstuffs are often brought in by helicopter, hence the relatively high charges made. But if you plan to undertake one or two multi-day tours in the mountains, the special atmosphere that comes from staying overnight in such remote lodgings will make the expense more than worthwhile. Membership of affiliated Alpine Clubs with reciprocal rights will give reduced overnight fees. (If you are a member of the U.K. section of the Austrian Alpine Club, for example, do not forget to take your membership card with you.)

Mention of any mountain hut, hotel or campsite in the main body of this book should not be taken as an endorsement of the services on offer.

MOUNTAIN FLOWERS

None but the most blinkered of visitors would fail to delight in the great variety of wild flowers on show in the meadows, woods and high, apparently barren screes of the Alps. The mountains and valleys of Central Switzerland, then, will appeal not only to botanists, but to all who gain particular enjoyment from sharing their walks with the rich flora of the hills. With summits over 3500 metres and valleys as low as 400 metres above sea level, it will be immediately evident that a number of vegetation zones exist here. Each has its own command of flowering glory.

Climatic contrasts are obvious, and these must also have an effect on the plantlife of the region. Consider the genial warmth of the lakeside. In summer·this can be almost Mediterranean-like, while on the mountains a day of snow or overnight frost may be expected at any time of the year. There are great contrasts too between mountain districts, and even from one side of a mountain to the other. Both the high basin at Melchsee-Frutt and remote Glattalp high above the Bisistal have large sections of limestone pavement that provide a habitat for plants very different from those that thrive at a similar altitude on Pilatus, or above the valley of Urnerboden, for example. At the southern end of the Urnersee the Reuss delta (now a nature reserve) displays a number of marsh-loving plants; again, so different from those tiny clusters of cushion plants that bring colour to otherwise mournful glacial moraines.

Valley meadows are particularly rich in wild flowers. I recall a walk in early summer that led through meadows outside Engelberg, a walk that became heady with fragrance. Another in the Maderanertal after a day of rain when the sun came out to cast a spell, drawing open blooms and filling the air with natural perfume. The Fellital is also rich in flowers, but get there before the goats are let loose on the hillsides.

Hillside shelves are good places to find wild flowers. One such is located high above the Schächental, another nearby, on the other side of the Klausenpass, where extravagant orange tiger lilies *(Lilium bulbiferum)* are found in early summer.

The stony upper reaches of the Göschener Tal, especially in the wild Chelenalptal, will surprise with the sheer variety of plants that are turning this former wilderness into a garden of beauty. There are plump mattresses of moss and golden marsh marigolds in damp areas. There are acres of alpenrose, and higher, starry alpines among the rocks, boulders and screes.

Practically every district and every level of altitude covered by this guide will repay the seeker of alpine flowers. This is not the place to enumerate or describe all those species you are likely to find, but there are several very fine identification books available that offer descriptions with lavish illustrations. Some of these are listed in the

Bibliography at the back of this guide.

A number of alpine plants are protected by law. A list of these varieties is regularly updated, and posters illustrating them are often displayed in railway stations, hotels and post offices. In addition there are a few nature reserves and Plant Protection Zones where the picking of any wild plant is strictly forbidden. Apart from such legal restraints the picking of flowers or collecting of plants may be seen as discourteous and inconsiderate, and can understandably breed resentment among local people. So please, walk in the valleys and round the mountains and be inspired and uplifted by the plants that you see. Study them, photograph them, breathe their heady perfume. But leave them for others to enjoy too.

MOUNTAIN ANIMALS

If an extravagant mountain flora colours our walks in Central Switzerland, it is the sighting of one or other of the wild denizens of the hills that can add a fresh dimension to one's days in the Alps. No-one who has managed to sit quietly and watch for several minutes as marmots carried on their marmot business unaware of your presence, will forget it. Nor will you easily dismiss from memory the experience of playing hide and seek with a chamois, or the joy of stumbling unexpectedly upon a group of ibex on a remote ridge. Such experiences may be conjured if you know where and how to look, how to walk quietly and to melt into the landscape at an opportune moment.

There are deer (red and roe) in the forests. Red squirrel, fox and Alpine hare are not at all uncommon, but of all mammals native to the Alps it is the marmot *(Marmota marmota)* that best represents the wildlife of the mountains.

Marmots, whose name comes from *Murmeltier* (the alpine mouse of the Romans) and the Central Swiss, *munkeln*, meaning secretive, are found in considerable numbers in the region covered by this book. Colonies of this furry little mammal, which grows to the size of a large hare and weighs anything up to ten kilograms, are located in many valleys, usually in the upper alps or among boulder slopes where there is plenty of cover for their burrows. These burrows are excavated with great vigour, the long front claws tearing at the soil which is then pushed away with the hind legs. In them marmots hibernate through the long winter months, emerging in springtime looking somewhat scruffy and scrawny, but ready to mate. Their young are born during the early summer, and you may be lucky enough to catch sight of two or three kitten-like creatures romping or playfully fighting in the short grass of the upper hillsides. Often the first indication a walker has of the proximity of a colony is the sound of a shrill warning whistle (in fact it is not a whistle but a cry from the throat) that appears to come from a sentry, seen standing alert and upright before racing for cover. In truth this sentry figure does not properly exist, except in fictional accounts, for it is merely the first animal to catch sight of potential danger that emits a warning. Sometimes it is not man's presence that gives cause for alarm, but the sight of an eagle or other bird of prey hovering overhead.

Should your attention be drawn to a colony by such a warning, find yourself a degree of cover and wait very still and quiet, and in due course your patience will be rewarded as the marmots once more emerge from the safety of their burrows. Unmoving objects will not normally be noticed at all, and you can quietly watch without being observed in return.

Chamois *(Rupicapra rupicapra)* are rarely seen at close quarters, being timid and elusive. But in the high mountain regions on or just below the snowline, it is not unusual to spy on a small herd picking a way with agile ease over excessively steep terrain. Except during the rut the chamois buck is a solitary creature, while females (doe) and their young roam together in herds of half a dozen or more. During the mating season several of these herds merge to form a considerable gathering.

Chamois, though shy and elusive, are more often seen than are ibex, or steinbock *(Capra ibex)* as they are also known. From a distance it is possible to mistake chamois, with their tawny coat and small curving horns, for female or young ibex. But ibex have a much stockier body (a full-grown buck can weigh 100 kilograms) and seemingly shorter legs, and they do not generally descend to the lower valleys. Rather they stay high, in very remote terrain, existing on whatever food plants they can find - even lichens. The buck grows long, sickle-shaped horns marked with a series of knobbles, which they use in battle as they fight for control over their herd. Normally they roam alone, like the male chamois, except during the rut - which is sometime between November and January. Hinds produce their young in early June, and within hours of birth the young ibex will be ready to follow their elders into the wild upper reaches of the mountains. Although I have watched a good number of chamois in the mountains of Central Switzerland, I have yet to see an ibex there.

WEATHER

The old adage, mountains make their own weather, is a truism acknowledged by all who have spent time walking or climbing in the Alps. Central Switzerland is no exception, and even within this one region there are a number of variations, a cocktail of micro-climates.

The high mountains of the Central Swiss Alps attract similar conditions to those of the Bernese Alps if, perhaps, a little better. Those conditions are notoriously volatile, since weather systems sweeping in across north-west Europe and the low Swiss plains have little to deflect them, so the high peaks act as conductors of rain clouds. Sudden thunder storms are not at all uncommon in summer. Summer precipitation below 2000 metres will be in the form of rain, while above that level snowfall may be expected. However, when the *Föhn* winds blow there will be clear skies for days at a time.

The *Föhn* is a warm, dry southerly wind blowing from the Mediterranean, and when it sweeps across the Vierwaldstättersee the lake whips violent waves and warning flashers along the lakeside should be heeded by anyone planning to take a boat ride or with ambitions for wind-surfing. The *Föhn* is felt at Altdorf on about forty-eight days of the year, and the effect it has on the higher mountains is quite dramatic, with a speedy melting of snow and a shrinking of glaciers. Following in the wake of this wind, rain may confidently be expected.

Temperatures are frequently dictated not only by elevation, but also by topographic configuration. Deep valleys, for example, may collect cold air at night but, protected from chill winds by day, their temperature range can be considerable. Average July temperatures vary from 18 degrees Celcius at Lucerne and Altdorf, to 14 degrees at Engelberg, though these temperatures are often considerably exceeded on still, wind-free days. Summer precipitation is around 53 centimetres (21in) at Engelberg, but 43 centimetres (17in) at Altdorf.

Daily weather reports are often displayed outside post offices and all major railway stations. Tourist information offices and mountain guides' bureaux usually have a barometer by which you can check pressure trends, while by dialling 162 it is possible to obtain an up-to-date weather report on the telephone.

June will normally be the earliest month to consider a walking holiday in the Central Swiss Alps, unless you plan to remain in the low valleys. Until late June some of the upper slopes should be avoided because of low-lying snow and even danger from avalanche. Late June/early July is the optimum time for flowers; August can be wet, but September is often settled and with the best opportunities for long walking tours. Though turning cold at night days are frequently bright and clear, while in October, if the weather holds, night frosts turn larch needles to gold and there is magic in the contrasts of colourful forests, snow-dusted hillsides and a deep blue sky. Many of the resorts, however, begin to close down for a few weeks before the winter season begins.

NOTES FOR WALKERS

In common with others in the series, this guidebook has been planned for use by walkers who may never have ambled through an alpine valley before, as well as by the more experienced mountain trekker aiming for the high cols and rugged inner recesses of glacier-hung peaks. There is something in the Alps for all to enjoy, and I am convinced from personal experience in Switzerland and elsewhere, that each level has its own spice, its own essential charm, its own rewards. Much of the pleasure of rambling among these mountains comes from the great variety of scenery that the paths lead through. That variety in Central Switzerland is enhanced by the character of the Lake of Lucerne that imposes its personality on a number of neighbouring districts. It may be experienced in the lowliest of valleys, as well as upon the upper hillsides among the very boundaries of heaven and earth. If the wanderer sets out with an eye for the views, for the flowers and shrubs in the meadows, the lichen-embroidered rocks beside the trail, for the crystal clarity of the streams and tarns and the dark mystery of the forests, he will never be disappointed with his day.

Naturally, the more adventurous the route planned, the greater must be one's preparation for it. The following brief notes have been assembled to aid that preparation, so to enable you to make the most of your visit to Central Switzerland.

Those who set out on a mountain walking holiday will gain the most from it if they are in fair physical shape upon arrival. The day you begin your holiday in the Central Swiss Alps is not the time to start thinking about getting fit! The best training for a mountain walking holiday is walking - uphill. Most regular ramblers will appreciate this and will have been taking exercise at home before the holiday, in order to avoid stiff aching legs and a pounding heart from tackling a strenuous outing without first getting body and limbs into condition. Don't make the mistake of taking on too much for the first day or so, but instead gradually increase height-gain and distance covered day by day. There should be sufficient outing suggestions contained within this guide to enable you to enjoy a good day out at any level. Certainly every valley, every hillside and grassy ridge has its own unique flavour to sample at will.

The next point to consider will be that of equipment, the choice of which can make or mar any walking holiday, at home or abroad. Boots, quite naturally, are of prime importance. They should have vibram-type soles, be comfortable and well-fitting, and broken-in before heading for the Alps. Several lightweight models are readily available and these will leave you less weary at the end of a day's walking than would the older, more traditional heavyweight variety.

Neither do they require much in the way of breaking-in. Mediumweight boots are also available on the market. These will give a little more support, perhaps, for use on screes, and are likely to offer better waterproof qualities than the ultra-lightweight kind. On low valley walks along beaten-earth paths, strong shoes or trainers should be adequate.

Shorts may well be fine to wear on most summer walks in the region, but full leg protection should be carried in the rucksack, particularly on routes that go high. Should the wind spring up, clouds descend or a storm appear, you will need to pull on something more substantial than shorts. A sudden breeze at 2500 metres can seem extremely cold, and even the temporary loss of the sun can create a dramatic lowering of temperature. Strong winds can arrive with little warning, and even in the height of summer a dusting of snow on the tops is not at all uncommon. Be prepared with warm waterproof clothing. At the very least a thick pullover should be worn or carried in the rucksack for low walks. Even when setting out on what is a bright summer morning, waterproof cagoule and windproof clothing should be packed if you intend going up onto the mountainside. Headwear and gloves are also advisable for multi-day tours.

If one needs to be protected against possible cold and wet conditions, the alternative extreme scenario of dazzling sun and unshaded heat needs addressing too. Sunglasses will help those prone to headaches caused by too much exposure to the sun, and a sun hat with a brim will also be useful. Because of ultra-violet rays the alpine light is often exceedingly bright, even on cloudy days, and those with sensitive eyes should on no account leave their sunglasses behind. Sunblock or high factor suncream should be used for skin protection. A lip salve is also useful. All these items are easily obtainable in resort shops in Central Switzerland.

A small day sack should be adequate to contain spare clothing and other necessary items such as basic first aid kit, map and compass, whistle, torch and spare batteries, drinks container and food, on most outings except multi-day tours when overnight equipment will need to be taken. Backpackers, of course, will need to carry camping and cooking gear. Use butane gas or liquid fuel stoves when wild camping. A box of matches or lighter ought to be kept handy, in order to burn toilet tissues in those instances when you're "caught out" in the mountains. Bury faeces well away from paths and water sources.

As for drinking water in the mountains, most streams above habitation level should be pure enough, unless sheep, goats or cows are grazing above. Although you are unlikely to suffer any water-related problems, to be safe you should treat all such water supplies with a certain degree of caution. Perhaps the safest course whilst out walking would be to limit topping up your bottle to those hewn-out log troughs that are frequently found in valley pastures. These are filled by spring-fed pipes whose gushing fountains should be perfectly safe to drink from.

For safety's sake never walk alone on remote mountain trails, on moraine-bank paths or glaciers. For those who prefer to walk in the company of a group and have not made prior arrangements to join an organised walking holiday, the staff of several tourist information offices arrange day walks in the company of a qualified leader. These take place throughout the summer and are often free of charge to those staying in the organising resort. Enquire at the tourist information office of your village base for specific details.

PATHS AND WAYMARKS

Most of the paths and tracks to be followed by users of this guide will be routes that have developed over the centuries by farmers or chamois hunters going about their daily business - from alp to alp, or from one valley to the next by way of an ancient pass, or up onto a ridge where chamois might be spotted. Some are historic trade routes, mule trails that have been in existence for many generations; some have been tramped by armies, or by priests travelling from district to district as part of their pastoral mission. A few have been made in comparatively recent times by the local commune, by a branch of the Swiss Footpath Protection Association, or by members of a climbing club in order to reach a mountain hut.

Officially-maintained paths fall into two categories, both of which are efficiently signposted and waymarked by paint flashes: the *Wanderweg* and *Bergweg*.

A *Wanderweg* is a low path that either remains in the valley itself or runs along the hillside at a modest altitude. They are well maintained and graded at a much more gentle angle than the *Bergweg*. Yellow metal signposts containing the names of major landmark destinations, such as a pass, lake, hut or village, are found at intervals along the trail. Signposts also give estimated times in hours *(Stünden,* or *Std)* and minutes *(Min)*. A white plate on these yellow signs gives the name of the immediate locality and, often, the altitude in metres. Along the trail occasional yellow signs or paint flashes on rocks or trees give assurance that you are still on the correct route.

A *Bergweg* is a mountain path which ventures higher and is more demanding than a *Wanderweg*. These paths will invariably be rougher, more narrow, and sometimes fading if not in regular use. Walkers using them should be properly equipped, for they lead to remote areas, often over rugged terrain. Signposting is similar to that for a *Wanderweg* except that the outer sections of the finger post will be painted red and white, and intermediate paint flashes along the trail will be white-red-white bands. There may well be the occasional cairn to offer additional route-finding aid where the path has faded away or crosses a boulder slope, and in the event of low cloud obscuring the onward route it is essential to study the area of visibility with great care before venturing on to the next paint flash or stone-built cairn.

SAFETY IN THE MOUNTAINS

Without wishing to be alarmist or over-dramatic, it is the duty of the guidebook writer to draw attention to dangers that exist for the inexperienced and unwary in mountain country. A sudden storm, stones dislodged from above, a twisted ankle on a scree-slope - each of these things could have serious consequences should the party be ill-prepared to cope with an emergency.

Some of the higher corners of the mountains covered by this book have few visitors, even in the height of summer. A sense of solitude gained when wandering in them is one of the benefits of the area, but with that solitude there exists an over-riding seriousness - especially for the lone walker. This is not country to indulge in long solo journeys, for even a relatively minor accident could develop into a major epic if third-party assistance is required.

Wandering along a valley path should present no difficulties, of course, but the higher one ventures in the mountains the more realistic the walker's approach should be. Walk carefully, be properly equipped, take local advice as to weather prospects and plan your day accordingly. Take care not to dislodge stones from the path, for they may fall onto another unfortunate walker, farmer or animal some way below. Path conditions may have been altered by storm, rockfall or avalanche since these route descriptions were written, and a trail that is wandered without concern by some may be perceived to be dangerous by others with less experience, or by those who may be out of condition (mentally or physically). Exercise prudence and use common sense in your judgement of a situation that calls for care. Never be too proud to turn back should you find that your chosen route takes longer than anticipated, or if it becomes difficult or dangerous. Watch for signs of deteriorating weather and study the map well in conjunction with your compass before visibility is reduced. Think ahead.

In the unhappy event of an accident, stay calm. Should your party be numerically large enough to send for help whilst someone else remains with the injured member, make a careful written note of the exact location where the accident victim can be found. If there is a mountain hut nearby, seek assistance there. If valley habitation is nearer, find a telephone and dial **01 383 11 11**. This calls out the Swiss Air Rescue - but *should only be used if absolutely necessary.*

The international distress call is a series of six signals (either blasts on a whistle or flashes by torchlight after dark) spaced evenly for a minute, followed by one minute's pause, then repeat with a further six signals. The reply is three signals per minute, followed by a minute's pause.

There is no free mountain rescue service in Switzerland, and though remarkably efficient, emergency rescues can be both extremely expensive to mount and costly for the victim or his family. Specialist mountain insurance companies often advertise in the climbing press, and some standard holiday insurance policies often include mountain walking in the Alps as one of the acceptable risks - although rescue will form no part of standard cover. Do check the small print for certain exclusion clauses. Be insured, and be cautious.

GRADING OF WALKS

Walks described in the following pages are designed to help you make the most of your holiday, and since it is intended that walkers of all degrees of commitment will find something of value contained within, it seems that a grading system might be useful in directing readers to the standard of outing of particular interest or appeal. Since grading is not an exact science the three categories used will cover a fairly wide spectrum. They follow a pattern set by previous alpine guidebooks in this series covering the mountain regions of Switzerland.

Grade 1: Suitable for family outings, mostly short distances involved or along gently-graded paths or tracks with little change of height to contend with.

Grade 2: Moderate walking, mostly on clear footpaths. Some will be *Wanderweg* paths, others *Bergweg* trails with some altitude gains. Walkers should be adequately shod and equipped.

Grade 3: More strenuous routes on rough paths. Some scrambling may be involved in rare instances. There may be high passes and also small snowfields to cross, some steep ascents and descents, possibly scree work and/or long distances involved. Walkers attempting these routes should be well equipped.

The Chelenalp Hut (Routes 65-67)
From the ridge high above Melchsee-Frutt you gaze into the Gental (Routes 76-77)

The Vierwaldstättersee (Lake of Lucerne) from Pilatus Kulm (Routes 25-28)
High peaks above the Hürital in Central Switzerland (Routes 35-36)

RECOMMENDED MAPS

Maps of the official Swiss Survey (*Landeskarte der Schweiz* - LS) cover the whole country and are magnificent works of art that will breed excitement into the heart of all map enthusiasts. Open any sheet and a picture of the country immediately leaps from the paper. By clever use of shading, contours and colouring, the line of ridges and rock faces, the flow of glaciers and streams, the curve of an amphitheatre, the narrow cut of a glen, the expanse of a lake and the forest cover of a hillside all announce themselves with welcome clarity. They are a source of inspiration prior to setting out, and a real pleasure to use in the mountains.

At the head of each valley section of this book a note is given as to the recommended map to use. In every case I have chosen the 1:50,000 series, as this should be adequate for most, if not all, the walks described. On the whole there is such good waymarking on the ground which for the most part does away with the need for greater detail than is to be found on these sheets. Clearly, more intricate detail is given on sheets at 1:25,000 scale, but rather a lot would be needed to cover the same area.

Six sheets in all at 1:50,000 cover the complete area described in this guide, and are listed below:

235	*Rotkreuz*	236	*Lachen*
245	*Stans*	246	*Klausenpass*
255	*Sustenpass*	256	*Disentis*

USING THE GUIDE

A brief word of explanation is offered with regard to the use of this guide and conventions adopted. Distances are given throughout in kilometres and metres, as are heights. (To convert kilometres to miles, divide the distance given by 1.6093; for metres to feet divide the amount given by 0.3048.) Measurement details are taken directly from the relevant map, but in attempting to establish the actual distance of walks described I have made the nearest estimation I could. With countless zig-zags on many routes it is impossible to be exact. Likewise, times are also approximate only and make no allowances for rest stops or photographic interruptions. Inevitably these times will be found slow by some walkers, fast by others. By comparing your times with those quoted here will soon enable you to form an idea of the amount by which we differ, and then make the necessary adjustments. Remember though, these routes are designed not for racing, but for a simple enjoyment of fine mountain scenery and in order to absorb the maximum of mountain experience.

In decriptions of routes, directions "left" and "right" apply to the direction of travel, whether in ascent, descent or traverse. However, when used with reference to the banks of glaciers or streams, "left" and "right" indicate the direction of flow, ie. looking downwards. Where doubts might occur a compass direction is also given.

A note too, about the word "alp". Commonly the Alps are taken to mean the chain of mountains spreading in an arc from the Mediterranean to the Julians of one-time Yugoslavia. However, traditionally "alps" were to the mountain peasants not the peaks themselves, but those high pastures on which cattle were taken to graze during the summer months on what was known as the *transhumance*. Some of the walks in this guide wander through alp hamlets, linking the high pastures with all their lush fragrance and idyllic views. They are indeed, alps among the Alps.

Finally, I have made every effort to check these routes for accuracy and it is to the best of my belief that the guidebook goes into print with all details correct. However, changes are made from time to time; paths are re-routed, certain landmarks altered. Any corrections required to keep the book up-to-date will be made in future printings wherever possible. Should you discover any changes that are necessary, I'd very much appreciate a brief note of the particular route and alteration required. Likewise, suggestions for additional routes that you may have found enjoyable, or recommendations that would help improve future editions. A postcard via the publisher would be gratefully received.

VIERWALDSTÄTTERSEE
(LAKE OF LUCERNE)

Position:	**North of the Central Swiss Alps, the Vierwaldstättersee is an irregular-shaped lake whose fingers spread south, east and south-eastward from the town of Lucerne.**
Maps:	**L.S. 235 "Rotkreuz" 1:50,000**
	L.S. 245 "Stans"1:50,000
	L.S. 246 "Klausenpass" 1:50,000
Bases:	**Lucerne (439m), Weggis (444m), Vitznau (435m),**
	Brunnen (435m), Sisikon (446m), Flüelen (439m),
	Altdorf (454m), Seelisberg (804m)
Tourist Information:	**Verkehrsbüro, Frankenstrasse 1, 6002 Lucerne (Tel: 041 51 7171)**
	Verkehrsbüro, 6353 Weggis (Tel: 041 93 1155)
	Verkehrsbüro, 6354 Vitznau (Tel: 041 83 1355)
	Verkehrsbüro, 6440 Brunnen (Tel: 043 31 1777)
	Verkehrsbüro, 6452 Sisikon (Tel: 044 2 1612)
	Verkehrsbüro, 6454 Flüelen (Tel: 044 2 4223)
	Verkehrsbüro, 6460 Altdorf (Tel: 044 2 2888)
	Verkehrsbüro, 6377 Seelisberg (Tel: 043 31 1563)

A holiday based in one of the many charming lakeside resorts on the Vierwaldstättersee (Lake of Lucerne) will provide the greatest variety of scenic attractions in the region, as well as the best opportunity to explore the surrounding area. The public transport network is superb, while for those with their own vehicle, a system of motorways enables a fast journey to be made from one end of Central Switzerland to the other.

Scenically the many fingers of the lake reveal contrasting aspects

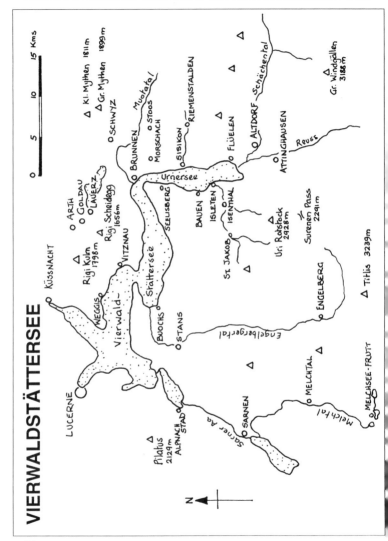

VIERWALDSTÄTTERSEE

of grandeur. The northern end is open and expansive and bordered by modest wooded hills. The southern spur, the Urnersee (Lake of Uri), is more dramatic and fjord-like, with close-ranged mountains rising from its east and west shoreline and with the Uri-Rotstock (2928m) claiming its share of the southern horizon. Water sports are popular. There's paragliding from several hilltop sites high above the lake; rack-railways and cableways give access to stunning viewpoints and allow gentle walks to be had in the most delightful of settings. There are undemanding lakeside walks and outings of a more strenuous nature available from any one of a number of resorts. And should the weather turn bad, Lucerne has enough attractions to keep you occupied - and dry.

The first mountain of note is the Rigi (1798m), a celebrated viewpoint with a large summit hotel and plenty of other accommodation and tourist facilities scattered about its slopes. Rigi is a broad block consisting largely of a knobbly form of conglomerate seen running in long bands between patches of forest and pasture. Chestnut and almond trees grow on its warm, sunny flanks and alpine flowers dazzle in early summer. To the north Rigi rises steeply, while to the south green terraces ease the slope. Cattle graze the pastures. Chamois and deer thrive where once the cave bear roamed - in full view of the sparkling lakes that form this very heart of Switzerland. Whilst not completely isolated as an island peak, lakes mostly surround it. The Küssnachtersee (a north-east projecting finger of the Lake of Lucerne) forms one of its boundaries, the Zugersee another, the smaller Lauerzersee a third, and the main extensive arm of the Vierwaldstättersee a fourth.

Not surprisingly the lake has attracted visitors for centuries. As early as 1585 the springs high up on the southern flank, where now the Kaltbad stands, were discovered to have healing properties. A hundred years later the chapel of Maria zum Schnee was built, and this soon developed into a place of pilgrimage. The first modest hotel was erected at Rigi Kulm in 1816 and from then on sunrise viewed from the summit became an important ingredient on the itinerary of every educated visitor to this part of the Alps. Goethe, Victor Hugo and Mark Twain are just three of those who fell for its charms. And who can blame them?

Summit views are indeed quite magnificent, not only at sunrise or sunset, and will repay a fine-weather visit. Cable-cars and cog railways from Weggis, Vitznau and Arth-Goldau may have replaced the sedan chairs that carried nineteenth-century visitors to the top, but the glory of the panorama has not changed and there are scores of trails winding round the mountain at all levels to reveal one intimate scene after another.

In 1897 Mark Twain stayed at the lakeside resort of Weggis, claiming it to be "the most charming place we have ever lived in for repose and restfulness". Vitznau huddles between the shoreline and the feet of the mountain a few kilometres to the south-east. From here the lake road gives a very fine and scenic journey of a further 14 kilometres as far as historic Brunnen, one of the most popular of resorts on the lake.

Behind Brunnen a broad, flat-bottomed valley cuts north-eastward to Schwyz, which is backed by the twin Mythen peaks, while directly across the lake on the nose of a steep promontory (the start of the Urnersee), stands the beautiful old boatman's house of Treib which was used as a meeting place by the early Confederates between 1637 and 1767. Round the corner a little from Treib is historic Rütli Meadow. Views from Brunnen, however, are dominated less by these individual features than by lofty mountains that plunge into the water, and from the town to Sisikon and on through the tunnels and galleries that score the Axenberg cliffs on the way to Flüelen at the lake's south-eastern corner (38 lake kilometres from Lucerne) it is the fjord-like aspect that gives additional charm to the scene. Behind Sisikon stretches the Riemenstaldner Tal that provides footpath access with the Muotatal.

Flüelen is busy with lake steamers and trains on the Gotthard line, yet it is not so well known as Altdorf, the main town situated 3 kilometres to the south which pays homage to William Tell. Altdorf is the capital of canton Uri; in the town square stands a bronze statue to the legendary Swiss hero, and during the summer local people re-enact Schiller's play which keeps Tell's name alive.

On the western side of the Urnersee there are no mainstream

resorts, but one or two charming villages sit tight against the soaring mountains. Isleten looks to the lake, and provides little more than a hint of the valley which cuts away behind it. This valley, the Grosstal, curves towards the Engelberg-Rotstock and is divided from the lesser glen of Chlital by the Uri-Rotstock. The Chlital flows into the Grosstal at the village of Isenthal a short distance upstream from Isleten.

Bauen is the next small village to the north. From it a splay of footpaths climb up onto the wooded slopes above (the hillside plunges so steeply into the lake that there is no shoreline to walk along), and makes a scenic link with Seelisberg that has funicular access with Treib on the water's edge opposite Brunnen.

As mentioned earlier the boathouse at Treib occupies the nose of promontory that effectively marks the northern limit of the Urnersee. From here the Vierwaldstättersee breaks away to the west. On its southern shore sit Beckenreid, Niederdorf and Buochs, the latter town set on an alluvial flat broken by the Engelberger Aa - the river draining, as its name implies, the valley of Engelberg. Above Buochs to the north, and protecting it from the winds, the 1000-metre Burgenstock rises straight out of the lake, its hotels creating a mini-resort reached by road and funicular.

Below the western end of the Burgenstock the Alpnachersee joins the Vierwaldstättersee as a narrow neck of water flowing between Stansstad and Hergiswil. The Alpnachersee, fed by the Sarner Aa, is walled by Pilatus, that other magnificent viewpoint which, in common with the Rigi, should be on the list of all visitors to the region.

From Alpnachstad at the southern end of the Alpnachersee, the world's steepest cog railway climbs to a saddle a few metres below the Esel peak, one of the summits of Pilatus, while a combination of gondola lift and cable-car reaches the same point from Kriens, a suburb of Lucerne. The mountain with its several summit points, the highest of which (Tomlishorn) is a modest 2129m, is a rugged, dominant mass which stands virtually isolated from its neighbours. This isolation is partly responsible for the extent of its panoramic views which are justifiably famous. They are, in fact, even better than those from the Rigi, and offer remarkable variety, including not only the sparkling lakes below, but the far-off blue line of the mountains of the Jura and Black Forest.

In the south-east the Urnersee leads the eye to peaks of the Glarus (or Glarner) Alps whose snow-washed summits include the Hausstock, Clariden and Tödi. This line of summits continues round to the Urner Alps (the Alps of canton Uri) and those that rise above Engelberg, including the jagged Spannort and more boldly-formed Titlis. But it is the great sawtooth of the Bernese Alps in the south and south-west that really excite the imagination: Finsteraarhorn, Wetterhorn, Mönch, Eiger and Jungfrau (appearing in unaligned disorder from this angle), the Breithorn, Tschingelhorn, Blümlisalp and Wildstrubel, fading and falling with distance beyond a foreground and middleground of green hills and rocky fins, of blue-shadowed valleys that in themselves hold much of appeal too.

The name of Pilatus is thought to derive from *Mons Pileatus*, the mountain capped with cloud, although it was generally known as *Fractus Mons (Frackimund)*, the broken mountain, until the fifteenth century. A superstitious ban on climbing the mountain was apparently imposed in the early Middle Ages, which resulted in punishment for six priests who attempted the climb in 1387. However, it is thought that the summit was reached sometime in the fourteenth century. Other ascents followed, but it was not until 1585 when Pastor Johann Muller led members of his congregation onto the mountain that superstition was finally dispelled. After this a steady number of locals and foreign visitors made the ascent. Queen Victoria was one who rode a mule to the top in 1868. The cog railway from Alnachstad was built between 1886 and 1889 and until 1936 it was operated by steam. Since then electrification has reduced the time taken to reach the summit from almost $1^{1}/_{2}$ hours to just 30 minutes. To walk, of course, takes considerably longer - about 4 hours in all.

Main Valley Bases:

LUCERNE (439m) retains much of its noted architectural charm despite a rash of uninspired modern development. Situated at the north-western extremity of the lake where the Reuss escapes (the river is spanned by attractive covered wooden bridges), it is the capital of its own canton and a popular commercial and holiday centre, although situated rather too far from the mountains to be a perfect choice as a base for a walking holiday. It has direct rail access with the airports of Zürich (65kms) and Geneva, while the N2 and N14 motorways converge on the town, thus providing a fast approach (and exit) by road. Lake steamers depart from the town's quayside near the railway station (*Bahnhof*). Lucerne has all the amenities of a large modern town, including a choice of museums, art galleries, theatres, cinemas etc. The full range of accommodation, from luxury hotels to youth hostel and campsite provide overnight lodging for more than 6000 guests. There are also holiday apartments for rent.

WEGGIS (444m) nestles below the Rigi on the southern side of a spur of land which effectively separates the arm of the Küssnachtersee from the main body of the Vierwaldstättersee. Rebuilt after being virtually destroyed by landslide in 1795, it is a small but popular resort with a resident population of about 3000, and is accessible by boat from Lucerne. Nearest railway station is Küssnacht (7kms), which is served by bus. A cable-car rises from Weggis to Rigi Kaltbad. The resort has beds for more than 1200 guests in hotels that range from unclassified to 4-star, plus 120 holiday apartments. Nearest approved campsites are at Küssnacht and Vitznau.

VITZNAU (435m) lies about 6 kilometres south-east of Weggis and is smaller than its neighbour with whom it shares fine views across the lake. There are a few shops and banks in the village, as well as PTT and tourist information office. In addition to holiday apartments (135 beds) there are ten hotels (1-5 star) providing accommodation for more than 700 guests, and there's a campsite at the southern end of the village. Vitznau is served by lake steamer from Lucerne and Brunnen. Buses link the village with the railway station at Küssnacht. The cog railway which runs from the lakeside to Rigi Kulm was built by Niklaus Riggenbach and inaugurated in 1871, making it the oldest mountain railway in Switzerland. Initially the line went only as far as Staffel (1603m), because the Schwyz cantonal authorities refused to grant permission for it to cross the canton's boundary, which includes the summit. (The Goldau to Rigi track, on the east side of the mountain in canton Schwyz, was opened just four years later, with the final stretch of track being leased to the Vitznau-Rigi line in canton Lucerne!)

BRUNNEN (435m) makes a popular base for holidays both active and inactive. Idyllically situated on a delta of land spilling into the lake at the mouth of the Muota, access by rail, boat or road puts a number of outlying districts within easy reach. Attractive walking country lies on its doorstep, while beautiful views are to be had both across the lake and to the mountains at the southern end of the Urnersee. As a resort Brunnen has a good selection of shops, restaurants, banks, a helpful tourist information office and PTT. There are twenty hotels and pensions covering all categories with some 1200 beds, and 250 beds in holiday apartments. Brunnen has two campsites, both situated on the northern side of the Muota.

SISIKON (446m) is caught midway along the Axenstrasse, an impressive piece of engineering where both road and railway have been tunnelled through the steep plunging cliffs of the Axenberg. The village is very small, with about 700 inhabitants, and is the most northerly in canton Uri. As a resort it has only limited facilities. However, it enjoys a fine outlook across the lake, while immediately behind it a gorge leads into the Riemenstaldner Tal, in which is found a remote community within canton Schwyz. The village has a railway station and is also accessible by lake steamer and Postbus (limited service to Rimenstalden). It has two hotels offering a total of 98 beds, and an invariably busy campsite.

FLÜELEN (439m) is situated at the southern end of the Urnersee below the cliffs of Eggberge, with which it is linked by cable-car. It has an important railway station on the Gotthard line, is regularly served by lake steamers and has Postbus links with Altdorf and the Klausenpass, as well as a service round part of the western side of the lake. There are shops, restaurants, tourist information office, banks and PTT. Three hotels (2- and 3-star) provide beds for 130 guests, and there is camping on a small terraced site on the lakeside.

ALTDORF (454m) lies south of the Urnersee at the foot of the road which climbs into the Schächental and over the Klausenpass. It is the capital of canton Uri, a small but busy town that makes much of the legend of William Tell. It has some attractive old buildings and a number of modern shops and restaurants, banks, tourist information and PTT. The canton hospital is also situated here. Altdorf's three hotels have beds for about 120 guests. A campsite is located just outside town at Moosbad.

SEELISBERG (804m) is set high above the west bank of the lake in a remote but beautiful position. It's a scattered, sunny community of about 600 inhabitants, reached by winding road from Stans and Beckenreid via Emmetten, or by funicular from the lakeside at Treib. (Tourist information at the upper station.) Fine walking country lies along the wooded heights to the south and west. The historic Rütli Meadow is found steeply below to the east. Seelisberg has just three hotels offering about 120 beds. There is a campsite at the tarn (Seeli) from which the village derives its name.

Other Valley Bases:

Practically every village and small town along the shores of the Vierwaldstättersee provides accommodation for visitors. The above list is selective, rather than comprehensive. In addition to lakeside resorts, there are delightful villages like **MORSCHACH** on a green shelf high above Brunnen, or **BURGENSTOCK** above Buochs that provide lodgings in magnificent settings. **ISENTHAL**, tucked away in a little valley behind Isleten on the western shoreline of the Urnersee, offers beds for 38 in one hotel well away from the crowds.

If you are prepared to move away from the Lake of Lucerne yet still be close enough to take advantage of the facilities on offer there, plenty of "inland" accommodation is available in and around Schwyz, and there are campsites at either end of the Lauerzersee.

THE RIGI (1797m)

No visit to Central Switzerland would be complete without a pilgrimage to the summit of the Rigi. Never mind the hype, the crowds, the buildings, the mechanical means of reaching this famed viewpoint, it is the glory of those views that ought to be claimed as an essential part of the holiday experience. If the Victorians "discovered" and extolled the beauties of Switzerland, we may yet echo their delight, and it doesn't matter if you have climbed some of the more remote summits in that view and felt privileged to have them to yourself, nothing can detract from the distant middle-mountain panorama that the Rigi affords. It is said that this panorama measures some 800 kilometres in circumference. Overlooking the glinting fingers of the lake you gaze far off to a line of snowpeaks stretching from the Tödi to the Blümlisalp, while midway between wooded green hills are dotted with alp hamlets and haybarns, in short, the quintessential Switzerland.

The ascent of the Rigi from one of several lakeside bases on the Vierwaldstättersee will rarely demand more than a few hours' exercise by way of excellent, well-signed paths. Routes on the eastern side of the mountain (from Arth, Oberarth or Goldau) will similarly require only a morning's effort. But in some ways it is preferable to take either cable-car or cog railway to the summit, enjoy the views at leisure, then walk slowly down - into the views, as it were - virtually every step of the way being enriched by scenic pleasures.

There are trains to Rigi Kulm (the summit) from Arth-Goldau or from Vitznau. Cable-cars operate from Weggis to Rigi Kaltbad (about 350 metres below the top), and another from Küssnacht to Seebodenalp (1031m), a green shelf below the steep northern crags of the mountain, from which a choice of paths lead to the summit. There is also cable-car service from Vitznau (Buholz) to Hinterbergen and to Wissifluh, and from Kräbel (759m) above Arth-Goldau to Rigi Scheidegg, a subsidiary summit (1656m) to the south-east of Rigi Kulm. With such a wide range of mechanical aids available it would be possible to explore many sides of the mountain by a combination of footpath, rail and cableway, each one exploiting different views.

Route 1:	Rigi Kulm (1798m) - Vitznau (435m)
Grade:	1-2
Distance:	9 kilometres
Height loss:	1363 metres
Time:	$2^{1}/_{2}$-3 hours
Map:	L.S. 235 Rotkreuz 1:50,000

The suggestion here is to take the train from Vitznau to Rigi Kulm (35 minutes) and then wander back down again, stopping at selected viewpoints to absorb the panorama. A superb day out can be gained in this way. The Vitznau-Rigi Bahn begins at the lakeside and is clearly signposted with plenty of car parking space nearby.

Within moments of a train disgorging its passengers at Rigi Kulm the summit becomes crowded, but on the way down you will gradually find space and peace restored. From the summit follow the descending path beside the railway line, signposted to Vitznau, as far as the Staffelhöhe station and hotel buildings (1550m; *accommodation*, *refreshments*) where you take an alternative path branching slightly right ahead and signposted to Weggis and Kaltbad. This is the so-called Höhenweg, a path which at first overlooks the steep slopes that plunge away to the west, then gives a magnificent panorama to the snow giants of the Central and Bernese Alps to the south. (Paragliding enthusiasts use this area as a launching site.) After descending in easy windings the trail then veers left for Rigi Kaltbad (1438m; *accommodation*, *refreshments*), a busy collection of hotel and station buildings.

From here the signposted path descends well to the right of the railway, between meadows, before returning to it and then crossing at Romiti (1195m; *refreshments*). Now on the left of the railway the path goes down through woods to Freibergen (1018m) and Grubisbalm (910m), dropping past steep meadows and farms perched upon them, still with superb views over the lake to the high mountains. The route is clearly signposted all the way to Vitznau which you reach by the parish church a few paces from the Rigi railway station.

Ascent Routes - from Vitznau:
The following routes are given in outline only. The popularity of the mountain, together with plentiful signposting, should make more detailed description superfluous.

Route 2:	Vitznau (435m) - Kaltbad (1438m) - Rigi Kulm (1798m)

Grade:	2
Distance:	9 kilometres
Height gain:	1363 metres
Time:	3 hours 45 minutes
Map:	L.S. 235 Rotkreuz 1:50,000

The ascent via Grubisbalm and Kaltbad, in effect reversing the same route described above, is one of the easiest on the mountain. It begins by the village church a little north of the railway station and heads along a side-street before a footpath winding among isolated chalets takes over. Clear signposting all the way. Refreshments are available at Romiti (1195m), Kaltbad (1438m), Staffelhöhe (1550m), Staffel (1603m) and at Rigi Kulm.

Route 3:	Vitznau (435m) - Unterstetten (1422m) - Rigi Kulm (1798m)

Grade:	2-3
Distance:	10 kilometres
Height gain:	1363 metres
Time:	3¹⁄₂ hours
Map:	L.S. 235 Rotkreuz 1:50,000

This alternative ascent route climbs to the ridge between Rigi Kulm and Scheidegg, where fine contrasting views are to be had. Below and to the north the Zugersee stretches into a low, soft landscape. To the east the smaller Lauerzesee has the twin Mythen peaks rising just beyond, while yet again the Vierwaldstättersee dominates all views to west and south.

Head away from the lakeside at Vitznau by a side street to Buholz, where the cable-car to Hinterbergen has its valley terminus. A trail climbs from here to St Antoni (819m) and a junction of paths. Take the route that heads up to Hinterbergen (1113m; *refreshments*), on to Glatti over pastures, followed by a long traverse of the Vitznauer Alp to Unterstetten (1422m) on the ridge where refreshments are available. A track on the north side of the ridge will now take you without difficulty to First (1453m; *refreshments*), with a final climb to Rigi Kulm.

Route 4:	Vitznau (435m) - Rigi Scheidegg (1656m)
Grade:	2-3
Distance:	6 kilometres
Height gain:	1221 metres
Time:	$3^1/_2$-4 hours
Map:	L.S. 235 Rotkreuz 1:50,000

Almost directly above Vitznau rises the peaklet of Dossen (1685m), one of several summits along the main ridge of the Rigi. To the east of Dossen is Rigi Scheidegg (1656m), reached by cable-car from Kräbel to the north and from Gschwand to the south-east. Views from Scheidegg are as magnificent as those from Kulm, and this ascent route from Vitznau gives an opportunity to enjoy them. The walk is steep in places, but if required it is possible to reduce the effort by taking the cable-car from Buholz to Hinterbergen.

Follow Route 3 as far as Glatti. Continue on the main trail towards Unterstetten, but then break away at a junction at Point 1446m on a signposted path leading to Rigi Scheidegg (*refreshments*). This final stage of the walk gains the ridge at Point 1546m to the west of Scheidegg, and you then wander along it, with those lovely views to either side, gaining the last 110 metres of height in little over 1 kilometre.

Descent to Vitznau by the same route will take about $2^1/_2$ hours.

Ascent Routes - from Goldau, Oberarth and Küssnacht:
A long and fairly strenuous ascent route leads from **GOLDAU** by a combination of road and footpath to **DACHLI** where a trail then

branches off round the flanks of the mountain to **PLATTENALP** on the northern side. The trail then slants steeply uphill to **ZINGEL** (1526m) and finally to **RIGI KULM**. This would be graded 3, taking about 4 hours in all.

A pleasant traverse of the mid-height slopes goes from **OBERARTH** to **STOCK** (992m) below the summit of Rigi Kulm on its northern side, then round to **SEEBODENALP** (2¹/₂-3 hours) from where either descend to Küssnacht by cable-car, or continue to the summit by the steep and twisting trail up the face, emerging at **STAFFEL** a little under 200 metres from the summit. From Oberarth to Seebodenalp, grade 2; all the way to the summit, grade 3 (total 5-6 hours).

From **KÜSSNACHT** to Rigi Kulm via **SEEBODENALP**, using the final part of the route mentioned above, is a 3¹/₂-hour walk, graded 2-3 on account of the steepness of the trail above Seebodenalp.

Other Walks on the Rigi:
The longest and most challenging walk hereabouts is the **HÖHENWEG** (high path) from **RIGI KULM** to **BRUNNEN**. This is a Grade 2-3 walk, and it will take about 7-7¹/₂ hours in all. From Rigi Kulm take the well-signed trail to Staffel, down to First and on the Felsenweg to Unterstetten, Hinterdossen and Scheidegg. Then by way of the Gatterlipass, over the Gurgenalp to Schwand and Timpel where you can either walk steeply down through woods to Brunnen, or descend by cable-car.

A combination of the **OBERARTH-RIGI** walk and the **HÖHENWEG** trail to Brunnen would give a rewarding two-day traverse of the mountain, spending the night at the Rigi-Kulm hotel.

These, and other walk suggestions, are outlined on the *Rigi Exkursionskarte mit Panorama* (a panoramic map) available from stations on the Vitznau-Rigi Bahn and elsewhere around the mountain. Kümmerly & Frey, the Swiss publishers of walking guides, have a guidebook (in German) devoted to the Rigi region (no. 3688 entitled *Vierwaldstättersee-Rigi*). It contains a number of route suggestions for the area and is on sale in local bookshops and, usually, tourist information offices.

THE SWISS PATH

The 700th anniversary of the founding of the Swiss Confederation was celebrated in 1991. One of the products of this anniversary is the *Weg der Schweiz*, the Swiss Path, which makes a horseshoe loop round the Urnersee from Rütli Meadow to Brunnen. It was conceived as a permanent reminder of the anniversary, a unique trail developed by, and on behalf of, the twenty-six cantons that make up the Confederation. Each of the cantons is represented by a stretch of the route, the length of which is in direct proportion to the population of that particular canton. At the beginning of each representative stretch of the walk a marker stone, in the shape of a Swiss cheese, is engraved with the name of the canton responsible, and the date it joined the Confederation.

The route is scenically delightful for much of the way with wonderful views of lake and mountain, meadow and forest. Unfortunately (a personal grievance) some of the cantons represented in the development of the path saw it as a promotional opportunity, and some hideous temporary adornments were stategically placed along the way. These did nothing to enhance the natural beauty of the walk, but rather detracted from it. My own hope is that such unnecessary features will disappear now that the anniversary year is over.

In its first year (it was inaugurated in May 1991) the route was, understandably, exceedingly popular with hordes of walkers tackling it in family groups, rambling clubs, school parties - and lots of individuals too. One might reasonably expect that numbers of users will fall off in the ensuing years, so that by the time this guidebook is published it should be possible to wander the Swiss Path other than in a disorderly procession! But let none of the foregoing comments dissuade you from tackling the Swiss Path. It's a fine walk.

The whole route is 35 kilometres long, but it could happily be broken into a number of separate walks. The Swiss authorities divide it into six separate stages. For the purposes of this book, however, it is written as two walks. Occasional timings are given, together with a note of the availability of public transport facilities along the way, so walkers can finish wherever they choose.

Marker stone on the Swiss Path

The start at Rütli Meadow may be reached by lake steamer from one of a number of resort villages, and there are several other convenient places similarly served by steamer that the path leads through, thus providing a romantic approach and finish to the walk. (A special 32-page guidebook, with panoramic sketch map, has been produced to promote the walk. An English language edition, *The Swiss Path*, is available from tourist information offices and bookshops around the lake.)

Route 5:	Rütli (482m) - Seelisberg (804m) - Bauen (436m) - Flüelen (439m)
Grade:	1-2
Distance:	19 kilometres
Height gain:	382 metres
Height loss:	428 metres
Time:	6-6½ hours
Maps:	L.S. 245 Stans and 246 Klausenpass 1:50,000

Rütli Meadow slopes towards the western shore of the Urnersee below the village of Seelisberg. Brunnen occupies the lakeside across the narrows to the north and it is from there that many walkers set out to tackle the Swiss Path. Steamers regularly make the short trip to Rütli by way of Treib.

Rütli has its own landing stage, and as you step ashore you will see the first of the special Swiss Path waymarks. This is in the form of a three-sided cross, the fourth side of which is an arrow. The waymark is painted on a yellow direction board identical to the standard *Wanderweg* signs. (Note that the arrow on the waymark is always pointing to the right, and should not be taken as an indication of the direction of travel.)

The Swiss Path rises through Rütli Meadow. As has already been mentioned, Rütli (meaning "clearing in the forest") is virtually a place of pilgrimage. It was bought by the State in 1859. There is a restaurant in a traditional building (the *Rütli Haus*) which stands near the top of the slope. The path then climbs in numerous zig-zags through forest to reach Seelisberg (804m; *accommodation, refreshments*), set on a grassy terrace overlooking the lake.

Heading through the village the route then enters forest once more at Oberdorf, with meadow clearings here and there that give surprise views. Coming out into the open again, waymarks lead along a quiet road where you can see down to the right to the small lake of Seelisberg Seeli set in a green valley of its own. Steeply uphill on a path you pass the handsome white building of Beroldingen Schlöss, originally built in 1500.

The path to Beroldingen reaches the highest point on the Swiss Path (864m). Now the descent to Bauen begins: a long, and at times steep, descent on an endless flight of steps between meadows and woodlands and with lovely views into the upper reaches of the Urnersee and the Reuss valley beyond. So reach Bauen (436m; 3 hours, *refreshments*) a pretty hamlet on the lakeside. For those who require it, there is a steamer service back to Brunnen and elsewhere.

The remainder of the walk to Flüelen traces the lake shore. Between Bauen and the hamlet of Isleten you pass through a series of tunnels with galleries blasted in the cliffs during the 1950s. Isleten

(435m *refreshments*) also enjoys a steamer service, as well as bus link with Flüelen.

From Isleten to Seedorf at the head of the lake the path is accompanied for a short distance by road, but then you cross through the nature reserve of the Reuss delta, an area of marshland with reeds and pools and watercourses busy with various ducks, coots and frogs. The path meanders through, edges the lake with its wash of flotsam, and enters Flüelen (*accommodation, refreshments*). A frequent steamer service from here enables a return to be made to your base. The village is also served by train (link with Brunnen, Schwyz etc) and bus (to Altdorf).

Route 6:	Flüelen (439m) - Sisikon (446m) - Morschach (646m) - Brunnen (435m)

Grade:	1-2
Distance:	16 kilometres
Height gain:	389 metres
Height loss:	393 metres
Time:	5 hours
Maps:	L.S. 245 Stans and 246 Klausenpass 1:50,000

This second stage of the Swiss Path remains throughout on the eastern side of the Urnersee. Although it is written here as a north-bound walk, there is a convincing argument for the route to be tackled in a south-bound direction, on account of the views. However, views are splendid too as you head above Sisikon towards Brunnen and the open expanse of the Vierwaldstättersee seen enticingly ahead. In fact there are many visual delights along the way, as well as items of interest, such as Tell's Chapel between Flüelen and Sisikon. Between Flüelen and Tellskapelle there are some steep climbs and descents, and a short section that leads through tunnels on the old Axenstrasse road. As with the first stage of the walk there are plenty of opportunities for refreshment along the route, and there are two steamer landing stages (at Tellsplatte and Sisikon). Morschach is linked by bus with Brunnen. Waymarking is superb throughout.

From the landing stage at Flüelen the Swiss Path is signposted along to Usserdorf, the northern end of the village, passing alongside the railway and turning right by the entrance to the campsite. Cross an inflowing stream, the Gruonbach, wander through trees and go up to the old Axenstrasse road with views over the lake. Shortly before descending to Tellskapelle (Tell's Chapel) you come to a barn-like building which houses a display of photographs.

Tellskapelle (436m) is open on its lake side and has a large graphic painting by Ernst Stuckelberg depicting the swearing of the Rütli oath, and three others illustrating scenes from William Tell's life. The chapel dates from 1879 and stands on the site of two previous chapels. Just beyond it the path brings you to Tellsplatte, a brief projecting spur of land where, it is said, the legendary hero leapt ashore and made good his escape from the boat carrying him off to prison. Tellsplatte has a restaurant and a landing stage for the lake steamers.

The onward path is a delight, and for much of the way it undulates a little above the shoreline, then climbs through woods to the road before descending once more, this time to reach Sisikon (2 hours, *accommodation, refreshments*). Sisikon enjoys a fine situation on a delta of land below the Riemenstaldner Tal, a sheltered spot with lovely views across the lake. (Steamer service to Flüelen and Brunnen; rail link also with Brunnen.)

Out of Sisikon the path now climbs through woods, steeply in places, then out into the open to Tannen (803m) where a glorious panorama is to be had. The way continues along a high shelf way above the lake, with meadows and isolated farms. After passing the seventeenth-century chapel of St Franz-Xavier in Hinterlauinen the descent begins to wind through meadows to Morschach (646m; 4 hours, *accommodation, refreshments*); a small resort village nestling in a bowl of hills above the lake. From here the path to Brunnen is mostly through woods, but with occasional fine viewpoints from which you can make out Seelisberg across the lake, and far off Pilatus and the Rigi.

BRUNNEN (435m)

Although Brunnen has mountains in view, the village is somewhat divorced from them and much of its attraction is owed directly to the lake. That being said there is some interesting walking country spreading away from it: not as demanding as several other areas described in these pages, perhaps, but certainly not lacking in charm. The following brief outline routes will give an indication of what is on offer. They represent just a small handful of the opportunities available to walkers. Staff at the tourist information office can provide a copy of the *Panorama Wanderkarte* with routes marked on it. The Kümmerly & Frey guidebooks in German which cover this area are nos. 3688 *Vierwaldstättersee-Rigi* and 3686 *Uri* available from local bookshops.

Route 7:	Brunnen (435m) - Morschach (646m)

Grade:	1
Distance:	3 kilometres
Height gain:	211 metres
Time:	1 hour 15 minutes
Map:	L.S. 245 Stans 1:50,000

This is a short, but nonetheless a pleasant walk to a small village set in a gentle bowl of meadowland, a shelf of hillside below the Fronalpstock (1922m) to the south of Brunnen. The route makes use of a combination of metalled road, woodland track and footpath, and is waymarked as for the Swiss Path (see routes 5 and 6 above).

The walk begins in the main street of Brunnen (*Bahnhofstrasse*) where it crosses a stream. Take the narrow side road which cuts off to the right (east) from the lake side of the bridge. Waymarks soon lead you up among houses, gaining height and into woodland, the Ingenbohlerwald. Although there are alternative woodland paths the trail to Morschach is clearly marked. It takes you past one or two viewpoints overlooking the lake, and eventually out of the tree shade and onto a quiet road leading directly into Morschach.

Morschach above the Vierwaldstättersee

Whilst here it is worth visiting the church of St Gallus which dates from 1509. Buses run from Morschach to Brunnen for the return.

Route 8:	Brunnen (435m) - Morschach (646m) - Stoos (1275m)

Grade:	2
Distance:	7 kilometres
Height gain:	840 metres
Time:	3-3$^{1}/_{2}$ hours
Maps:	L.S. 245 Stans and 246 Klausenpass 1:50,000

Stoos is a small winter and summer resort tucked on a terrace to the east of the Fronalpstock, and is one of those delightful places free from motor traffic. In summer its Fronalpstock ski-lift is adapted as a chairlift, thus enabling walkers to gain height easily and then wander the high trails with stunning views, reckoned to be almost as good as those from the Rigi. Although Stoos is politically linked with Morschach, visitors normally make their way to it via Schattli in the Muotatal where a funicular provides access. This walk, however, is an extension of Route 7, and it leads you to Stoos by way of wooded slopes from the easy meadows of Morschach.

Take the trail to Morschach as outlined as Route 7. Near the church find the path signposted to Dagenbalm (720m). From there the way skirts the lower edge of forest, rising gently with views to the Mythen peaks above Schwyz, then begins a more direct ascent of the tree-lined slopes to the north of the Fronalpstock. Ascend steeply, so to gain the terrace of Stoos.

Route 9:	Brunnen (435m) - Morschach (646m) - Sisikon (446m)

Grade:	1-2
Distance:	8 kilometres
Height gain:	393 metres
Height loss:	382 metres
Time:	3 hours
Map:	L.S. 245 Stans 1:50,000

The Swiss Path is described above as Routes 5 and 6. This particular walk is in fact a reversal of part of Route 6 but is offered here as a reminder that some wonderful views are on show from that terraced shelf between Morschach and Sisikon, which might otherwise be missed by those who consider the full Flüelen-Brunnen stage too long to tackle as a whole. Refreshments are available at Morschach, and the return to Brunnen from Sisikon could be comfortably achieved either by lake steamer or by train.

Follow outline directions from Brunnen to Morschach as per Route 7. Continue following Swiss Path signs heading south on a narrow metalled road which rises easily and rounds a hillside spur at Schilti. The Sisikon trail wanders along a delightful terrace with long views ahead over the lake and to the high mountains that wall the Reuss valley. Beyond Tannen (803m) the way soon begins its
56

descent among forest shade, and leads directly to Sisikon.

Route 10:	Brunnen (435m) - Schranggigen (448m) - Ranggen (930m) - Lauerz (457m)

Grade:	2
Distance:	7 kilometres
Height gain:	495 metres
Height loss:	473 metres
Time:	3¹/₂ hours
Map:	L.S. 235 Rotkreuz 1:50,000

North of Brunnen, hidden away in a lovely broad and gentle valley with its own lake, is the village of Lauerz. The village and its lake are separated from the main valley of the Muota by a long ridge spur running from the Rigi. At the point where it forms a wall to the Muota valley this spur is known as the Urmiberg. The walk outlined below crosses the Urmiberg and gives an opportunity to witness the different aspects of the valleys on either side.

Brunnen with the Mythen behind

From Brunnen railway station cross to the western side of the Bahnhofstrasse and walk along the narrow Wilenstrasse to Wilen, a suburb of Brunnen on the true right bank of the Muota and tucked at the foot of the Urmiberg. Continue along the road to Schranggigen - there should be very little traffic. On reaching Schranggigen take the trail that climbs over meadows and into woods to reach an inner hanging valley at Brunniberg. From here the climb continues and tops the ridge at Ranggen (930m). The descent to Lauerz is made by a combination of footpath, track and metalled road.

Lauerz has two campsites (on the road to Goldau), and another at the eastern end of the lake. Return to Brunnen by bus.

ALTDORF (454m)

Mountains overlook this capital of canton Uri, but the Urnersee is just too far to the north to be part of its charm. Instead it relies on history and legend for its character. It has a town atmosphere and with plenty of shops and museums for wet days, while there are good public transport facilities to enable walkers without their own vehicle to reach some splendid outlying areas. Of particular note are the Isenthal valleys on the west bank of the lake, and the Schächental/Klausenpass region rising above to the east, both districts being described elsewhere. A few long walks begin virtually on the edge of Altdorf, which sits astride the route of that classic trans-Switzerland walk, the Alpine Pass Route.

Route 11:	Altdorf (454m) - Eggberge (1447m)
Grade:	2-3
Distance:	7 kilometres
Height gain:	993 metres
Time:	3 hours
Map:	L.S. 246 Klausenpass 1:50,000

Eggberge (or Eggbergen) is a region of alpine farms and chalets set amid sloping pastureland high above the valley. The mountain walls that support this pastureland are uncompromisingly steep above Altdorf, and the historic forests of Banwald which clothe the slopes immediately behind the town are preserved to safeguard it against avalanche. A cable-car rises from the outskirts of Flüelen to Eggberge, enabling skiers in winter and walkers in summer to enjoy its lofty position and its far-reaching views. This walk, briefly outlined, points to an alternative ascent: one that is a little energetic, but nevertheless rewarding as it heads mostly through the Banwald forest.

It begins near the church of St Martin, north-west of the *Rathausplatz* (marked by Kissling's bronze statue of William Tell), where a *Wanderweg* signpost directs the way to Planzeren and Eggberge, soon on a narrow metalled road heading through the Banwald to Unter Planzeren (638m). At Mittel Planzeren (695m) break away to the right, heading south-east for about 15 minutes. At a junction of tracks head left to Ober Planzeren (898m), the middle station of the Flüelen-Eggberge cableway. The way continues to climb through forest, steeply in places, and then emerges by the top station at Eggberge.

Return to Altdorf by the same route or to Flüelen by cable-car. An alternative option is to make a very full day's outing by heading slightly north of east from the Eggberge top station to cross a col by the little tarn marked Flesch on the map. Continue from there round the head of three corries before descending steeply over meadows and past a number of alp buildings to reach Spiringen in the Schächental (4 hours from Eggberge; grade 2-3). Catch the Postbus from Spiringen back to Altdorf.

Route 12:	Altdorf (Gitschenberg; 1369m) - Gitschital - Seedorf (452m)
Grade:	2
Distance:	11 kilometres
Height loss:	917 metres
Time:	3½ hours
Map:	L.S. 245 Stans 1:50,000

To the west of Altdorf, on the far side of the Reuss valley, the mountains rear up as a lovely, seemingly unbroken wall. First impressions are that this wall is vertical and almost impregnable. Yet the upper slopes are dotted with alp farms and there are some delightful minor valleys draining the peaks. Through farm and hanging valley wind several paths. From them the mountain walker gazes at one enchanting scene after another. Cableways provide easy access to these upper regions; one from Seedorf to Gitschenberg, another from Oberdorf (Seedorf) to Rüti, and a third from Attinghausen to Brüsti. Both Seedorf and Attinghausen may be reached by bus from Altdorf. (At Seedorf, near the cable-car station, there's a small but picturesque gabled castle dating from the sixteenth century and named A Pro after the Ticinese mercenary leader who built it.)

Take the cable-car from Seedorf to Gitschenberg. From the top station wander south along the path which makes a traverse of the pastures below the rocky peak of Gitschen (2540m) and in about half an hour brings you to the alp buildings of Honegg (1421m). Beyond Honegg you enter thick forest where the trail gradually loses height as it goes deeper into the Gitschital.

On reaching the alp farms of Gitschitaler Boden (1296m; 2 hours) bear left and follow the valley path down through the Gitschital, keeping above the left bank of the Palanggen stream. The trail remains mostly among trees, comes to the Rüti cableway station and soon after makes a determined descent to the valley with a number of tight zig-zags.

Route 13:	Altdorf (Gitschenberg; 1369m) - Gitschital - Chli Laucheren (1820m) - Brüsti (1525m)

Grade:	3
Distance:	8 kilometres
Height gain:	525 metres
Height loss:	295 metres
Time:	4-4½ hours
Map:	L.S. 245 Stans 1:50,000

This walk links two cableways separated by the valley of the Gitschital and a ridge spur running north-east from the Brünnistock. Grand views down to the Urnersee and across the Reuss valley towards the Klausenpass are just part of the pleasures gained.

Follow route 12 into the Gitschital at Gitschitaler Boden (2 hours). Instead of heading downstream continue towards the head of the valley and cross the stream to its right bank near Distleren (1526m). The trail now forks. One branch strikes up pastures to cross the spur to Chli Laucheren (1820m); the other, left-hand, option heads north-eastward to cross the spur at a lower point before doubling back on its southern side to reach Chli Laucheren (3 hours 15 mins) by a more devious route. From here head south and join the Surenen Pass trail which you follow downhill to the chalets of Brüsti *(accommodation, refreshments)*. Take the cable-car down to Attinghausen in the valley (the descent by steep footpath takes 2 hours from Brüsti).

Route 14:	Altdorf (Brüsti; 1525m) - Surenen Pass (2291m) - Engelberg (1002m)
Grade:	3
Distance:	20 kilometres
Height gain:	766 metres
Height loss:	1289 metres
Time:	7 hours
Map:	L.S. 245 Stans 1:50,000

An important section of the Alpine Pass Route (a 16-pass walk from Sargans to Montreux), this is a magnificent outing, one of the very best to be had in the mountains of Central Switzerland. It provides a strenuous day's walking, but there are many delights to be won: exquisite views, tarns, crags and snowspattered mountains, waterfalls, alp farms, an idyllic white-walled chapel. There are opportunities for refreshment on the way, and one or two remote *Matratzenlagers* should you be tempted to stop for the night before reaching Engelberg.

The Surenen Pass is a saddle in the ridge which links the Blackenstock and Schlossberg. From it the walker has a grandstand view of two contrasting landscapes, but eyes are held by the cluster of little tarns below on the western side, and by the snow-gleam of the Titlis that seems to dominate the valley down which you will walk to reach Engelberg.

Ride the cable-car (in two stages) from Attinghausen to Brüsti. (Attinghausen has hotel accommodation, while the chalets at Brüsti offer refreshments and accommodation, some with *Matratzenlagers*.) On leaving the top station you will see a signpost directing the route to the Surenen Pass. The trail passes a few chalets and heads along a crest among alpenroses and dwarf pine trees, edges a rocky section (hand rail) and soon after gains a splendid green ridge (Grat) with the Urnersee coming into view far below to the north.

Rising along the Grat ridge you will come to a saddle known as Nussfruttli (1953m; 1 hour 45 mins) from which you can see the Surenen Pass ahead. The path forks. Both branches lead to the pass, which is gained after a climb of about 45 minutes.

Unfortunately the descending path does not stray to the tarns seen below the pass, instead it swings well to the left of them. But they make a perfect site for a picnic, so it might be worth going down to them, and later find your way back to the path itself.

The descending trail is clearly defined, swinging down in lazy windings through a green but contorted landscape, arriving at Blackenalp (1773m *Matratzenlager, refreshments*) an hour below the pass. The solitary farm of Blackenalp is protected by a fine amphitheatre of mountains to the north. Nearby stands an attractive whitewashed chapel. Continuing, the route descends from one level to the next, passing a waterfall and with Titlis growing in stature ahead. Off to the left, as you descend towards Stäfeli, the rocky pinnacles of the Spannorter can be seen.

Berggasthaus Stäfeli (1393m) also has *Matratzenlager* accommodation and refreshments for sale. The path wanders directly past it and half an hour later comes to another alp farm offering refreshments. This is Alpenrösli (1258m; 5 hours), and it is here that you join a farm track. Engelberg lies about two hours farther down-valley. The track leads to a metalled road which heads through the valley to Engelberg. There are footpath short-cuts that can be taken here and there.

Seewen - tarns below Surenen Pass - Titlis in the background

Engelberg has a campsite and plenty of hotel accommodation. It is described in more detail below, with a number of walking routes suggested, under the section entitled Engelbergertal.

For more information and full route description of the Alpine Pass Route (Sargans to Montreux) consult the guidebook with the same name, published by Cicerone Press.

Route 15:	Altdorf (Brüsti; 1525m) - Nussfruttli (1953m) - Waldnacht - Attinghausen (469m)
Grade:	3
Distance:	19 kilometres
Height gain:	428 metres
Height loss:	1484 metres
Time:	6 hours
Maps:	L.S. 245 Stans and 246 Klausenpass 1:50,000

This demanding circular walk will make very good use of a day in the hills, and provide many features of interest. Care will be needed in certain places, however. Scenically delightful, it will nonetheless be extremely tiring on account of the long and steep descent to the Reuss valley. If preferred it would be possible to reduce this amount of descent by breaking away from the downward path just east of the Waldnachter tarn and wandering 100 metres or so up to Brüsti in order to catch the cable-car back to Attinghausen.

Take the cable-car from Attinghausen to Brüsti and follow the Surenen Pass trail described above as Route 14. When you reach the junction of paths at Nussfruttli (1 hour 45 mins from Brüsti) take the left-hand option and, at the next alternative, left again to descend alongside a stream to Eifruit (1781m) where a very steep descent (care required) is made into the head of the Waldnacht valley. Walk down through the valley to the small reservoir near the farms of Waldnachter (1402m). If you prefer to ride the cable-car back down to Attinghausen take the upward path, signposted to Brüsti. If not, continue beyond Waldnachter where the path soon enters forest and picks a steep zig-zag route down the hillside to Attinghausen, which it reaches near the valley station of the Brüsti cableway.

GOTTHARD ROUTE

Before leaving Altdorf mention should be made of the Gotthard Route - a 50-kilometre walk through the Reuss valley to Andermatt and Hospental, before heading over the St Gotthard Pass to Airolo in canton Ticino. This route hugs the river for much of the way and, despite traffic on the nearby road, has a certain attraction in that it follows a major historic route; one of the most important of all across the Alps. The Uri canton authorities publish a leaflet (in German) which describes the walk in some detail. Enquire at the tourist information office in Altdorf (or Andermatt) for the *Gotthard Wanderweg* leaflet. The route is briefly outlined below in three stages (as per the leaflet).

Äsch and its waterfall (Klausenpass section)

View to Firner Loch from Läcki (Rioutes 46-47)
Walker approaching the Fellilücke (Route 58)

Route 16:	**Altdorf (454m) - Amsteg (526m)**

Grade:	1
Distance:	13 kilometres
Height gain:	72 metres
Time:	3¹⁄₂ hours
Maps:	L.S. 246 Klausenpass and 256 Disentis 1:50,000

The walk really begins in Flüelen, but when started in Altdorf it is easily joined across the valley at Attinghausen by a thirty-minute stroll. Altdorf to Amsteg makes a very easy first stage.

From Attinghausen the path leads south on the true left (west) bank of the Reuss. At Ripshusen it joins a minor road to Erstfeld. Continue on the west bank until a bridge leads across to the eastern side at Tagerlohn, a short distance from Silenen. Amsteg lies at the mouth of the narrow Maderanertal another two kilometres upstream. Overnight in Amsteg (Hotel Stern & Post; 40 beds), or take the train from Amsteg-Silenen back to Altdorf.

Route 17:	**Amsteg (526m) - Gurtnellen (928m) -**
	Göschenen (1102m)

Grade	1-2
Distance:	16 kilometres
Height gain:	576 metres
Time:	5¹⁄₂ hours
Maps:	L.S. 256 Disentis and 255 Sustenpass 1:50,000

On this section of the Gotthard Route the walk crosses the Reuss on three occasions. It follows footpaths, tracks and roads. At the southern end of Amsteg a track is taken along the east bank to Vorder Ried and Meitschligen (672m; 1 hour 30 mins). The west bank is followed to Gurtnellen and Wiler (2 hours 50 mins), but on the outskirts of Wassen (where the lovely Meiental breaks away towards the Susten Pass) you return to the east bank again. A footpath then leads through valley pastures for nearly an hour, but at the Wattingen bridge a final return to the west bank is made. Göschenen is reached in another hour or so. This village, at the entrance to the magnificent Göschener Tal, has two hotels (1-star Gotthard with 44 beds; 3-star Zum Weissen Rössli with 55 beds). It also has rail access with Andermatt and Altdorf.

Route 18:	Göschenen (1102m) - St Gotthard Pass (2108m) - Airolo (1175m)

Grade:	2-3
Distance:	24 kilometres
Height gain:	1006 metres
Height loss:	933 metres
Time:	7-7½ hours
Maps:	L.S. 255 Sustenpass and 265 Nufenenpass 1:50,000

This makes a strenuous day's walking. The terrain under foot is alright, but there's a lot of ground to cover. Once over the Gotthard, however, the soft light of Ticino and the sea of snow-free peaks stretching either side of the Valle Leventina shows that this is indeed the southern flank of the alpine watershed; so different from the Central Swiss Alps you've just left behind.

Between Göschenen and Andermatt the Reuss gorge is a dark and gloomy defile, but when you emerge from it at Andermatt after 1½ hours, the Urseren valley opens ahead with a welcome display of space. Hospental is reached about 40 minutes beyond Andermatt, and the ascent to the pass then begins. Heading south follow the road to Gamssteg where you find the path which leads up alongside the Gotthardreuss to the canton boundary. Once over this you have entered Ticino.

The St Gotthard Pass (2108m) is gained after 4 hours 50 minutes. Plenty of opportunities for refreshment here, if you don't mind the crowds. Then follows the two-hour descent to Airolo, with the long trench of the Valle Leventina scoring a line through the mountains ahead. An intriguing sight.

Note: The Alps of Ticino offer superb walking in wild, secluded inner valleys, over gentle passes, linking numerous tarns or charming Italianate villages. For ideas see the guidebook *Walking in Ticino*, published by Cicerone Press.

Airolo has Postbus and rail services back over the pass or through the Gotthard Tunnel into Central Switzerland once more.

ISENTHAL (771m)

Draining the glaciers of the Uri-Rotstock and its neighbours the Grosstal and Chlital converge at the village of Isenthal. The Isitaler Bach then flows out to the Urnersee by the hamlet of Isleten. This the first and only real valley on the western side of the Urnersee is a somewhat wild and charming place of uncluttered innocence. The Postbus from Altdorf (30 mins) serves Isenthal and, at the roadhead, St Jakob. A cable-car rises from St Jakob to Gitschenen, an inner basin of pastureland with a couple of walker's passes breaching the upper ridges with routes leading to the Engelbergertal. At the head of the Grosstal, on the western slopes of the Uri-Rotstock beside the glacier of Blüemlisalpfirn, sits the Gitschenhöreli Hut: a privately-owned mountain refuge with room for about fourteen. (There is no guardian, and enquiries about its use - and availability of key - should be made to Eduard von Matt in Altdorf; tel: 044 218 76.) For accommodation in Isenthal enquire at Hotel Urirotstock, 6461 Isenthal (tel: 044 691 52). This unclassified hotel has 38 beds. Of the many walks and walking tours possible from the valley, the following brief outlines are but a sample.

Route 19:	Isenthal (771m) - Bauen (436m)

Grade:	1
Distance:	4 kilometres
Height gain:	120 metres
Height loss:	455 metres
Time:	1½-2 hours
Map:	L.S. 245 Stans 1:50,000

This short and easy walk would make a day's highlight for holiday-makers based elsewhere on the lake. One could start the morning, for example, by taking the Postbus from Altdorf to Isenthal, spend time looking at the valley, then walk to Bauen and catch a steamer back to Flüelen, and a bus from there to Altdorf. There are, of course, numerous options available.

From the church in Isenthal follow the narrow lane which rises along the hillside heading north-east (towards the lake). It leads through beechwoods and comes to a splendid viewpoint (Bärchi) overlooking the Urnersee above Isleten. Rounding the spur of land descend to Unter Cholrüti and walk into Bauen.

Route 20:	Isenthal (771m) - Furggelen (1222m) - Scheidegg (1386m) - Isenthal

Grade:	2
Distance:	6 kilometres
Height gain/loss:	615 metres
Time:	3½ hours
Map:	L.S. 245 Stans 1:50,000

Behind Isenthal to the north rises the modest wooded block of Scheidegg. At the western end of this mountain block is Furggelen; at the eastern end, Bärchi. This popular outing makes a part-circuit of Scheidegg and offers good views of the valley and its mountains as well as the lake.

Go up to Furggelen by a steep path on the edge of woods. (There is a cableway too.) Take a path heading to the right from Furggelen which makes a steady rising traverse of the northern side of Scheidegg, then descends steeply at the eastern end to reach the Bärchi viewpoint. Follow the narrow lane down to Isenthal.

Route 21:	Isenthal (771m) - Musenalp (1486m) - Sassigrat (1868m) - St Jakob (990m) - Isenthal

Grade:	3
Distance:	13 kilometres
Height gain/loss:	1097 metres
Time:	5-5$\frac{1}{2}$ hours
Map:	L.S. 245 Stans 1:50,000

A long ridge running north of the Uri-Rotstock effectively divides the Chlital from the Grosstal. In the middle of this ridge the Sassigrat presents an opportunity for the walker to link the two valleys, thus creating a fine, demanding day's exercise.

From Isenthal strike south along the Chlital by footpath and farm road. Near the end of this a path heads steeply up the right-hand slope to gain Musenalp *(accommodation, refreshments),* about two hours after setting out. The Sassigrat is now some 380 metres above and to the north-west. Reach this in another 45 minutes and descend on the western side by a path which slants leftwards down to Biwald (1694m) where there is a *Gasthof (accommodation, refreshments).* There is a junction of trails. Take one of those heading down into the valley, then follow the easy route through the Grosstal to St Jakob (4$\frac{1}{2}$ hours, *refreshments*) and back to Isenthal.

| Route 22: | Isenthal (771m) - Sinsgauer Schonegg (1924m) - Oberrickenbach (894m) |

Grade:	3
Distance:	14 kilometres
Height gain:	1153 metres
Height loss:	1030 metres
Time:	6-6$\frac{1}{2}$ hours
Map:	L.S. 245 Stans 1:50,000

Sinsgauer Schonegg is one of the walker's passes that provides a way from the Grosstal to the Engelbergertal. This particular route is rather strenuous but delightful.

Head upvalley from Isenthal to St Jakob (1 hour), then work your way up the western slope by an easy-graded trail that forks near the entrance to the Sulztal. Follow signs for the Sulztaler Hütte and Sinsgauer Schonegg. Cross the Sulztaler Bach on a clear route to the Sulztaler Hütte (1600m; 3 hours). From here the climb to the pass, seen above to the west, will take about an hour. Descend on the far side by a path which goes down the Sinsgau pastures, beneath a cableway, and reaches Oberrickenbach about 2 hours 15 minutes from the pass.

Oberrickenbach has a Postbus service to Wolfenschiessen in the valley. From there you can catch a train either to Engelberg (then return to the Urnersee on foot across the Surenen Pass) or to Stans and Lucerne.

Other Walks from Isenthal:
The above are just a few suggestions for the walker based in Isenthal. Both **HINTER-JÖCHLI** (2105m) and **STEINALPER-JÖCHLI** (2157m) above **GITSCHENEN** provide challenges with routes leading over the mountains to either the Vierwaldstättersee or the Engelbergertal. Less strenuous walks may be had in the Gitschenen meadows, or for those with climbing experience, an ascent of the Uri-Rotstock from either the Chlital or Grosstal. Study the map for more ideas.

SEELISBERG (804m)

Idyllically situated on the eastern flank of the peninsular whose projection into the Vierwaldstättersee effectively creates the separate arm of the Urnersee, this sunny village has much to commend it as a quiet base for a short walking holiday. Although it is easily reached by lake steamer via Treib or Rutli, and by Postbus from Stans, Seelisberg is not bothered by passing motor traffic. The road to it from Stans goes nowhere, except back to Stans. All around are forests and meadows with views over the lake. The Seeli tarn is cupped in its own gentle bowl; nearby stands Beroldingen Castle (it doesn't look at all like a conventional castle, but is more like a feudal *schloss*) and the hamlet of Bauen lies below to the south. Rising to the south-west of the Seeli tarn is the Niderbauen-Chulm (1923m), with a very fine panorama from its summit. Seelisberg comprises two parts;

Chilendorf, linked by funicular with Treib, and Oberdorf at its upper, southern end.

Route 23:	Seelisberg (804m) - Niderbauen-Chulm (1923m)

Grade:	2-3
Distance:	6 kilometres
Height gain:	1119 metres
Time:	3½ hours
Map:	L.S. 245 Stans 1:50,000

Since May 1991 when the Swiss Path was inaugurated (see Routes 5 and 6) abundant waymarks have effectively made it impossible to lose the way between Seelisberg and Beroldingen (or, indeed, anywhere along the path to Flüelen or Brunnen). Follow then the Swiss Path signs that lead towards Beroldingen (1 hour). Just after joining the path above the road north of the castle (where you have views down to the tarn on your right) take the trail heading uphill to Weid and Lauweli. It's a steep route, and the 400 metres or so of ascent to Weid (1288m) will occupy a good hour. The upper alp of Lauweli (1524m) is reached in 3 hours from Seelisberg, and another thirty minutes of effort will bring you onto the summit. Lovely views overlooking the Urnersee and the massed mountains to the south, west and east. Allow a minimum of 2½ hours for the descent by the same route.

An alternative way down, which would effectively make a traverse of the mountain, would be to descend on the north-western side to Tritt and Sagendorf, and then a short stroll to Emmetten (linked by Postbus with Seelisberg). This descent would take about 3 hours.

Route 24:	Seelisberg (804m) - Hoch Flue (1043m) - Sunnwil (771m) - Treib (435m)

Grade:	2
Distance:	13 kilometres
Height gain:	239 metres
Height loss:	608 metres
Time:	4¹⁄₂ hours
Map:	L.S. 245 Stans 1:50,000

This is an interesting circuit, mostly through forest and with surprise views of the Vierwaldstättersee. It finishes at the historic lakeside building of Treib from where you can take the funicular back to Seelisberg.

The path begins in Oberdorf a short distance south of the seventeenth-century chapel of Maria-Sonnenberg. It branches away from the road off to the right and heads into woodland, climbing to the Hoch Flue in a little under an hour. Continuing on a forest track the route swings west and south to Ober Schwand (910m 2 hours), then trends westward for about 45 minutes, losing height still, and comes out of tree-shade at the hamlet of Sunnwil (771m *refreshments*). Now take the trail heading north. It soon enters forest again and veers to the right to Stackenmatt where you join a quiet road. Follow this until you come to a path breaking away below, marked to Volligen (good views over the lake). From Volligen (508m *refreshments*) it is only a short stroll to Treib *(refreshments)*.

Other Walks from Seelisberg:
Plenty of short and easy and moderately-demanding walks may be enjoyed from Seelisberg. The above two scantily-described routes are perhaps among the best, but they are not the only long outings available. A six-hour walk, for example, takes you south to **BAUEN** as described under Route 5 (Swiss Path), then to **ISENTHAL** (a reverse of Route 19), down to **ISLETEN, SEEDORF** and **ATTINGHAUSEN**. A grand walk, graded 2-3.

The Swiss Path to **FLÜELEN** is another obvious walk to follow, and is described as Route 5.

Much shorter is the descent to **RÜTLI** (30 minutes or 1 hour, depending which path you follow) and trail from there to **TREIB**. From Treib return to Seelisberg either by funicular, or by a further hour's walk on a climbing path.

PILATUS (2129m)

As has been said of the Rigi, so might be said of Pilatus: a journey to its summit should be on the itinerary of all holiday-makers to the region. Rising above the western extremity of the Vierwaldstättersee, and standing back from the mainstream groups of alpine peaks, a veritable procession of shapely mountains lines up for inspection on the southern horizon. From this famed viewpoint so much of Central Switzerland (and the neighbouring Bernese Alps) is on show; it allows an unravelling of valleys and mountain massifs, but at the same time inspires as many questions as it provides answers. Go there at the beginning of a trip and you'll be fired with enthusiasm for the days ahead. Go there at the end of your holiday and you will have all the pleasures of recent days drawn into sharp relief.

There are two hotels (Hotel Kulm and Hotel Bellevue) just below the Esel summit.

As with the Rigi, the summit of Pilatus may be effortlessly reached by cog railway from Alpnachstad, or by cableway (gondola and cable-car) from Kriens on the outskirts of Lucerne. The mountain is also laced with walking trails from the four quadrants, of course, and the following route suggestions will provide a few ideas. A *Pilatus Wanderkarte*, giving route descriptions (in German) is on sale in shops, tourist information offices and railway stations in the neighbourhood. The Kümmerly & Frey *Wanderbuch* number 37, *Obwalden*, provides further routes, also in German.

Route 25:	Pilatus Kulm (2067m) - Ämsigen (1359m) - Alpnachstad (435m)

Grade:	2
Distance:	6 kilometres
Height loss:	1632 metres
Time:	3 hours
Map:	L.S. 245 Stans 1:50,000

Many visitors prefer to ride to the summit of Pilatus and walk down. This, the first walk described on the mountain then, is a descent route. It makes a splendid outing, but it is rather strenuous and, since the trail is very steep in places, it is somewhat tiring for the knees. Good footwear is essential.

If you take a morning train from Alpnachstad to the top station (thirty minutes) you'll have plenty of time to walk up to the Esel summit (2120m) a few minutes above the Hotel Bellevue for a wonderfully varied panorama. Also walk up to the Oberhaupt (2106m) above Hotel Kulm and wander round the gallery walk which affords surprising views. The highest of Pilatus's many tops, Tomlishorn, is reached in about twenty minutes via the *Panoramaweg* heading south-west from Hotel Kulm.

The descent to Alpnachstad begins immediately below the Pilatus Kulm hotel, a clear zig-zag path with red and white waymarks. At first a stony trail heading south, it soon leads to a grassy saddle where the way forks (Chilchsteine; 1865m). Bear left, soon to resume a zig-zag descent below the crags of the Matthorn (2041m). (The right-hand path descends to Lütoldsmatt to the west of Alpnachstad - see Route 28 for an ascent by this path.)

Soon come to an undulating basin rich in wild flowers and with a small stream flowing through it. The path swings to the right (south-east) and draws level with the railway. Following the railway line among trees, come to Ämsigen (1359m; 1¹/₂ hours) and a junction of paths. Continue downhill with the railway still on your left, and reach another fork. Bear left (always following directions for Alpnachstad) and soon enter the forest that clothes much of the lower slopes of Pilatus.

Crossing the railway when it enters a tunnel, the descent drops steeply to the north-east before easing a little and swinging right (still in forest), eventually coming to a narrow tarmac farm road. Leave the road just after passing a farm, and continue by footpath, once more through forest, until just above Alpnachstad where you cross through meadows, then by a series of steps down to Alpnachstad station.

Route 26:	Pilatus Kulm (2067m) - Tomlishorn (2129m) - Feldalp (1701m) - Wängen (1571m)

Grade:	3
Distance:	7 kilometres
Height gain:	62 metres
Height loss:	496 metres
Time:	$3^1/_2$ hours
Map:	L.S. 245 Stans 1:50,000

A very fine ridge-walk, for experienced mountain walkers only, this route traces the south-west ridge of the mountain. *Bergweg* waymarks throughout, but special care is required between the summit of the Tomlishorn and Widderfeld.

From Pilatus Kulm take the *Panoramaweg* to the Tomlishorn, highest point on the mountain and a splendid viewpoint (20 minutes). The route to here is not difficult, but as the ridge curves round the head of a steep corrie west of the summit it becomes rather more delicate. Cut round the western slopes of the Widderfeld and resume on the ridge (easier now) to the saddle of Feldalp ($1^1/_2$ hours). Beyond this the way rises over Rot-Dossen (1776m) to the Mittagsgüpfi (otherwise known as the Gnepfstein; 1917m), reached in about $2^1/_2$ hours. The ridge curves south-westward and the route descends along it to reach the Tripoli Hut (1800m; 3 hours), at which point drop southward to the alp of Wängen.

An easy route leads south-east from here to Lutoldsmatt (1149m; *Matratzenlager*) in one hour, and Alpnachstad in a little over two hours.

Route 27:	Alpnachstad (435m) - Ämsigen (1359m) - Pilatus Kulm (2067m)

Grade:	2-3
Distance:	6 kilometres
Height gain:	1632 metres
Time:	4-4½ hours
Map:	L.S. 245 Stans 1:50,000

This is the most direct ascent route from the south and is, in effect, the reverse of Route 25 above. It begins beside the Pilatus Bahn (the cog railway station) in Alpnachstad, which is close to the mainline (Brünig-Lucerne) railway station. There is a large car park nearby.

Climb a flight of steps to the left of the station building, then cross meadows heading north-east, under the railway line and into a patch of forest. Joining a farm road follow this for a short distance before breaking away left to climb on a forest trail. The ascent is not too demanding at first, but having passed beyond a line of crags the path swings left and makes a steep zig-zag climb, emerging on the edge of the forest by the railway line. Still gaining height steeply come to Amsigen (1359m) after about two hours.

Continue uphill beside the railway line to Mattalp, an open pastureland bowl, where the trail now swings left and climbs again in tight zig-zags below the Matthorn's cliffs. North of the Matthorn the busy summit of Pilatus can be clearly seen. Watch for paragliders who regularly make their colourful take-offs from the slope immediately below the summit hotels.

Route 28:	Alpnachstad (435m) - Lütoldsmatt (1149m) - Pilatus Kulm (2067m)

Grade:	2
Distance:	10 kilometres
Height gain:	1632 metres
Time:	5 hours
Map:	L.S. 245 Stans 1:50,000

A longer route than the more direct path described above, it is, however, a popular one and with fewer severe sections than Route 27. For those with their own transport it is possible to drive as far as Lütoldsmatt (from Alpnach), thus saving about $2^{1}/4$ hours of walking. There is *Matratzenlager* accommodation for 25 at the *Bergwirtschaft* at Lütoldsmatt.

The route begins by Hotel Rössli in Alpnachstad, heads south-west at first among houses, and rises to join a narrow road at Point 555m. Walk up the road (footpath short-cuts at several hairpin bends) to Lütoldsmatt (1149m; 2 hours 15 mins; *accommodation, refreshments*). The road forks. Take the left-hand option and soon after break away to the right on a footpath. This rises to Fräkmünt (1499m) about one hour after leaving the road. Now heading north-east make a steady ascent of the slopes below the Tomlishorn to gain a saddle at Chilchsteine (1865m; 4 hours 15 mins) where you join another path. Bear left and climb the last section to Pilatus Kulm.

Other Ascent Routes:

Trails converge on Pilatus Kulm from **HERGISWIL** in the east via **BRÜNNI** and **GSCHWAND** ($4^{1}/2$-5 hours); from the Eigental to the north-west, with trails starting from **EIGENTHAL** (1025m) and **UNTER LAUELEN** (1063m), and others from **KRIENS** to the north. It would also be possible to link several paths to create a multi-day circuit of the mountain. Study the *Pilatus Wanderkarte* for more ideas.

MUOTATAL

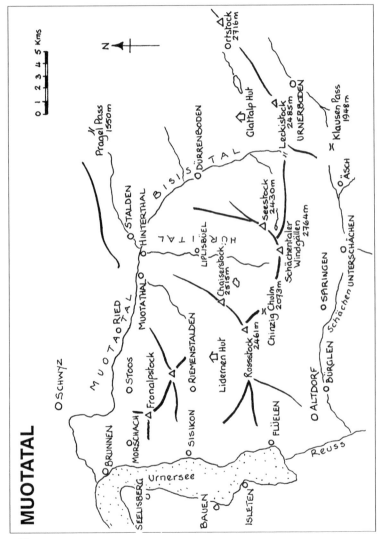

MUOTATAL

Position:	**East of the Vierwaldstättersee, in canton Schwyz**
Maps:	**L.S. 236 Lachen 1:50,000**
	L.S. 246 Klausenpass 1:50,000
	Schwyz (516m), Muotathal (619m)
Tourist	
Information:	**Verkehrsbüro, 6430 Schwyz (Tel: 043 21 3446)**
	Verkehrsbüro, 6436 Muotathal (Tel: 043 47 1515)

The valley of the Muota River is a gentle, flat-bedded trench steeply walled by green forested mountains. It's a quiet valley hidden away from the main tourist areas that surround the Lake of Lucerne, although the Muotatal is well-enough known to Swiss walking enthusiasts for whom the wide variety of routes of all grades of seriousness, particularly in its upper reaches, are of considerable appeal.

The Muota rises among limestone mountains that form the boundary between cantons Schwyz and Uri at the head of what is known as the Bisistal. Glorious country, that is, with wild peaks, ragged ridges, exquisite stretches of limestone pavement, tarns and waterfalls and soft valley pastures. There are no resorts in the Bisistal and no real villages as such, just a couple of small hamlets (Schwarzenbach and Dürenboden) and a scattering of alp farms. Ideal country, in fact, to explore on foot.

At its lower end the Bisistal is squeezed into a dark, wooded narrowing that opens again just to the east of Hinterthal, a hamlet that almost connects with the main village of the district, Muotathal. Two other valleys converge at Hinterthal. The valley of the Starzlen drains down from the north-east, while the Hürital enters the main Muotatal from the south.

Take the Starzlen first. A narrow road winds up into this forested valley and eventually reaches the Pragel Pass (1550m) beyond which lies the Klontal and the town of Glarus. (The north-eastern side of the pass is not open to traffic at weekends.) Off this minor road soft flower-rich pastures, marshy in places, lie cupped below a long wall of grey stone peaks. There are some fine walks to be had among them. But near the mouth of the valley, about two kilometres from Hinterthal, can be found the entrance to the Hölloch Caves; extensive caverns whose labyrinthine passages are estimated to reach inside the mountains more than 90 kilometres, only a mere fraction of which are open to the public.

As for the Hürital, this too is a gem approached by a serpentine road that is really little more than a farm service road climbing out of Hinterthal. Where this road ends footpaths continue to inner regions of some charm. One of these is a high undulating pastureland, the Seenalp, with a small lake caught within it. Above the lake to the north and west stands a guard of honour of peaks with the stature of misplaced Dolomites, topped by the Chaiserstock (2515m). Above Seenalp a ridge runs north-west to south-east, the southern flanks of which slope into the Schächental. In the midst of this ridge is the historic pass of Chinzig Chulm, crossed in 1799 by the 70-year-old Russian general, Alexander Vasilyevich Suvorov, and his army of 18,000 foot soldiers and 5000 horsemen. The remarkable journey made by Suvorov on his way to join the combined forces of Russian and Austrian troops at Zürich is a tale worth telling.

During the closing years of the eighteenth century both Russians and Austrians were attempting to drive the French revolutionary army of occupation out of Switzerland. In September 1799 Suvorov and his forces found themselves cut off by the French army, and in a desperate attempt to reach Zürich from Altdorf he forced three high passes in ten days. The first was the Chinzig Chulm (2073m), but when he reached the Muotatal he found the French already there, and after a two-day battle for command of a bridge down-valley, he set off over the Pragel Pass (1550m) to Glarus. From Glarus Suvorov and his men headed through the Sernftal to Elm, but again the French were there too. His only hope now was to escape over the Panixer Pass (2407m). However, by this time it was October, there was no marked route and the pass was covered in snow. But Suvorov and the remnants of his army managed to fight their way across, and 16,000 men reached safety on the far side.

Not surprisingly Suvorov and his exploits form part of the folklore of the region, and his name now appears in a number of different landmarks.

The Muotatal and its tributary valleys have few inhabitants. The combined resident population is a little over three thousand, and the only real village is Muotathal itself. (In 1900 this had a population of 2223.) At its lower, western end, the valley opens to the broad and sunny plain of Schwyz which, with its lovely cherry orchards, is backed by the Mythen peaks. Schwyz is the key to the outside world. As capital of its own canton it has rail access with Lucerne, Zürich and the Gotthard route, and a local private operator runs a bus service from the town through the Muotatal as far as Dürenboden/Schwarzenbach in the Bisistal.

Main Valley Bases:

SCHWYZ (516m), although not located in either the Muotatal or any of its feeder valleys, is nevertheless near enough to make a base for walks in the district, especially for those with their own transport. (As mentioned above, there is also a bus service into the valley from here.) The town has several attractive buildings dating from the sixteenth- to eighteenth-centuries. Pride of place goes to the highly decorated seventeenth-century *Rathaus* which dominates the central square. Nearby the Baroque parish church of St Martin, built by the brothers Jakob and Johann Anton Singer between 1769 and 1774, is considered to be one of the finest in all Switzerland. The town has all modern amenities and has some good walking country virtually on its doorstep, even without entering the Muotatal. (Of especial interest are the trails which lead up to and around the Grosser and Klein Mythen.) The town's hotels can accommodate about 160 visitors. Nearest campsite is on the shores of the Lauerzersee to the west.

MUOTATHAL (619m) is the principal village of the valley, all other habitations being little more than hamlets. Built as a ribbon of development alongside the road, a few blocks of buildings stand to the north of the road, between it and the river. There are few shops and little in the way of amenities for tourists. The combined accommodation list for this and the upper valleys amounts to no

81

more than about 170 beds in seven hotels. But there is a youth hostel in Muotathal catering for fifty members. The village has a seventeenth-century convent (founded 1280) and an eighteenth-century rococo church. In 1799 Suvorov made the village his temporary headquarters.

Other Valley Bases:
Accommodation may be found elsewhere in the Muotatal in the village of **HINTERTHAL**. In adjacent Hürital *Matratzenlager* lodging is available at **LIPLISBÜEL** some way short of the road-head. In the Bisistal there are gasthofs at **DÜRENBODEN** and **SCHWARZENBACH**, and at the head of the valley it may be possible to rent a room at **SAHLIALP**, near the Sahli-Glattalp cable-car station.

Mountain Huts:
Two huts of the SAC *(Schweizer Alpen Club)* are accessible from the Muotatal: the **LIDERNEN HUT** and **GLATTALP HUT**.

The **LIDERNEN HUT** (1727m) belongs to the Mythen Section based in Schwyz and is located on the northern side of the Rossstock, above the Riemenstaldner Tal, but is also reached by a $3^1/2$-hour walk from Hinterthal. The hut can sleep 86 in its dormitories. There is a guardian from mid-June to the middle of September when meals may be provided. The telephone number for bookings is 043 31 2970. From the hut climbs are made on the Rossstock, Chaiserstock, Fulen, Hundstock etc. One or two challenging walks may also be attempted from here. Among them the crossing of the Rossstock-Chaiserstock ridge to Seenalp and Chinzig Chulm.

The **GLATTALP HUT** (1898m) is approached from the Bisistal. It stands above an area of limestone pavement overlooking the Glattalp and is well-situated for a variety of long walks. Like the Lidernen Hut this too is owned by the Mythen Section. It can sleep 60, and the guardian is usually in occupation at summer weekends when meals may be provided. At other times self-cooking facilities are available. Telephone: 043 47 1939.

THE BISISTAL

The longest of the Muotatal's tributaries, the Bisistal is really the upper, south-eastern end of the main valley; a pastoral district through which streams run crystal clear between meadows bright with wild flowers. At its head it is enclosed by a knot of peaks, the Schächentaler Windgällen (not to be confused by the better-known Windgällen peaks to the south, on the ridge between the Brunnital and Maderanertal). The Höch Windgällen (2764m) throws out an arthritic choice of ridges and spurs roughly northward, while the main eastward-trending ridge forms the headwall of the Bisistal and also the northern limit of the Schächental, and is breached by two or three walkers' passes. Above the Klausenpass (which links the Schächental and Urnerboden) this boundary ridge then veers north-eastward for about 10 kilometres before giving out on the flanks of the Ortstock (2717m). Whilst the knotty Windgällen peaks form one cornerstone of the Bisistal, the Ortstock forms the other.

In reality the 10-kilometre wall referred to above effectively contains the hanging valley of Glattalp (served by cable-car from Sahli), a limestone scoop whose waters find an outlet in secretive subterranean leakings near the head of the Bisistal. But streams that drain the Windgällen opposite, and the rough pastures of Ruosalp below the boundary ridge, have no secrets to hide and come pouring down the hillsides in jubilant sprays, cascades and booming waterfalls. Of particular note is the huge waterfall fed by the Ruosalper Bach, considered by Baedeker (who called it the Waldibach Falls) to be the finest in Central Switzerland.

The bed of the upper valley is rich pastureland. Cattle graze the open meadows and amble to and fro across the narrow service road. There are shelves of pasture on the hillsides too, with isolated alp farms tucked away from the world, but as the valley drops in a series of steps to Schwarzenbach and Dürenboden, so forests darken the lower hillsides, while the valley bed itself becomes marshy in places.

Throughout, the Bisistal is an enchanting valley that will repay the explorations of walkers for whom the little-known and little-trod rather than crowded familiarity, hold particular appeal.

Route 29:　　　　Schwarzenbach (955m) - Vord Hütten (1330m)
　　　　　　　　　　- Milchbüelen (1353m) - Schwarzenbach

Grade:	2
Distance:	10 kilometres
Height gain/loss:	475 metres
Time:	4½ hours
Map:	L.S. 246 Klausenpass 1:50,000

Alp farms, lively streams, a lovely mountain tarn, curious rocky towers, long views - these are just some of the ingredients of this circular walk that will make a good introduction to the valley. In early summer there will also be a riot of alpine flowers as a bonus. One patch of meadow near the Waldi tarn is particularly rich in orchids - enjoy them, but please do not pick.

The start and finish of the walk is given as the hamlet of Schwarzenbach where the bus terminates, but it could as easily be Sahli at the roadhead near the Glattalp cable-car station where there is a small car park. If you plan to start there, simply walk down the narrow tarmac road for about 1.5 kilometres to Point 1092m (on the map) where the path starts on the left (west) of the road.

From Schwarzenbach follow the main valley road uphill for a little over 1 kilometre as far as Point 1092m. A rock on the right-hand side of the road bears a painted sign for Waldialp. *Bergweg* waymarks (white-red-white) lead uphill quite steeply at first over grass slopes and soon develop as a proper footpath which varies in clarity. In about 30 minutes from the road you will come to the alp huts of Vordersten Hütten (1330m) and join a farm track. This continues uphill, rising gently to the south, and 10 minutes later passes two more huts (Steinhütte; 1390m). Wander on with glorious views to the mountains that block the head of the valley.

Soon descend to a tarn sunken amid pastures. The track leads along the left-hand side of it and forks at the southern end. Take the left branch, in effect continuing ahead. Bear left over a concrete bridge and come to a junction of tracks at Ruosalp (1550m). Here you bear left again, but take the upper track (signposted to Klausen); a few paces later it forks again and you take the left option once more which leads to a large cattle byre/farm building.

Pass this on your left. Immediately beyond it the track veers to the right. After crossing a substantial stream the track deteriorates, but you continue along it. It finally ends at another stream, but about 50 metres before it does so leave the track and descend left on a narrow path (waymarks) which heads steeply down to the right of a lone hut. The path improves, bears right and crosses a stream on a wooden bridge at 1384 metres.

Over the bridge continue ahead, contouring along the hillside. The path is faint at times, but waymarks should form a clear enough guide. Eventually you come to a major path (it heads up to Glattalp) where you descend to the left a short distance to join a track. As you do so a grand view is afforded across the valley to the superb waterfall fed by the Ruosalper Bach.

On the track bear right and wander along it up to the alp of Milchbüelen (1353m). Pass beyond the alp buildings (signposted to Feldmoos) into an inner pastureland with a lovely stream flowing through. At the stream there is a choice of paths. Continue ahead on the way to Feldmoos (15 minutes from here). Waymarks take you up a slope a short distance to join a proper path which winds round along a high shelf of hillside to Feldmoos. Passing the alp building well to your left you join a farm road which forks soon after.

If you are returning to Schwarzenbach stay with the farm road as it snakes along the hillside, gradually descending to the valley. If, however, you have parked a car at the head of the valley, leave the road just before the fork and descend steeply to your left following a line of waymarks towards a solitary farmhouse. Just before this come onto a track and bear left. It will take you to the dam at the northern end of the Bisistal lake a short distance from the cable-car station.

Route 30:	Bisistal (Sahli; 1149m) - Ruosalper Chulm (2178m) - Balmer Grätli (2218m) - Sahli

Grade:	3
Distance:	12 kilometres
Height gain/loss:	1069 metres
Time:	5 hours
Map:	L.S. 246 Klausenpass 1:50,000

At the southern end of the Bisistal an amphitheatre of peaks (only two of which rise above 2600 metres yet give an impression of greater stature) embrace the hummocky pastures of Ruosalp. Above the alp snow lingers in shadowed gullies and chamois haunt the secret upper ribs and curvatures of the mountains. Though rarely guessed from below there are walkers' passes among these mountains which allow access from the Bisistal to the Schächental, Klausenpass and Urnerboden on the southern side. From east to west these are the Firner Loch (2248m), Balmer Grätli (2218m) and Ruosalper Chulm (2178m). The first leads to Urnerboden in 4-4^1/$_2$ hours, the second to the Klausenpass in 4 hours, and the third to several destinations in the Schächental. The walk offered here, however, is a circular one which links the two lower passes and offers fine views and rich contrasts.

Note: An important point to make about this fine wild circuit is that when it was being surveyed for inclusion in this guide, the path which links the two passes (Ruosalper Chulm and Balmer Grätli) on the southern side of the ridge had just been swept by a minor landslip which effectively destroyed a section of it. The route is being offered here with the assumption that the path has been recreated. Should you find that this is not so, however, my advice would be to descend back to the Bisistal by the upward route, as to continue in the hope of locating the path as marked on the map could be extremely hazardous. A there-and-back route would still provide a rewarding day out.

From the Bisistal road-head near the cable-car station cross the stream to the right bank and follow the farm road that winds uphill through woods. After about 15 minutes it forks. Continue straight ahead and a few paces later, when it veers to the right, leave the road and strike up the left-hand hillside on a faint path to the left of a stream. Coming to a bridge cross the stream, then head up the hillside again on a continuing line of waymarks that leads to a track. Bear right and wander along the track to reach a large cattle byre. Pass along the left-hand side of this and at a junction of farm roads turn left and head up to Unter Stafel, a small alp hut at 1496 metres.

The trail goes along the left-hand side of the hut and continues behind it, rising up the hillside for about 10-15 minutes when you cross an insignificant stream flowing into a deep gully on your right. The path is clear and obvious, but note that, at this stream crossing, a line of waymarks heads up the left-hand slope towards another small building. This is the path to Balmer Grätli by which our route will descend towards the end of the walk.

Continue on the obvious path to enter a high rolling pastureland. Head directly across it and twist up the rough grass slopes beyond. (Waymarks in lieu of a clear path for much of the way.) Above this short climb you come to a marshy basin and skirt it to the right, then rise over a series of grassy hillocks burdened with an over-abundance of dock leaves. The route now leads through a stony region with a good path, but this peters out and waymarks again direct you, now heading south across a grassy hillside. Over a stream, and above you to the left you see the spiky craglets of Rau Stöckli (2290m). The way now veers south-south-west and steepens towards the pass, twisting up towards the ridge before swinging left along a succession of marker poles and reaching the Ruosalper Chulm ($2^1/_2$-3 hours from Sahli).

The pass is an obvious saddle set in a craggy ridge. Immediately below on the south side there is a small tarn and the path to the Schächental descends easily to it.

Two paths branch left along the ridge. Take the upper path, narrow and without waymarks, but clear nonetheless. It rises along the ridge, first on the left, then on the right-hand side to traverse below the crags of Point 2318m. You will come to a narrow grassy saddle where you go left with a view down towards a solitary hut. The path is narrow, faint in places and sometimes exposed, but in thirty minutes from the Ruosalper Chulm, without losing too much height on the traverse, you should come to Balmer Grätli (2218m), a stony pass from which a waymarked path descends south to the Klausenpass.

Cross the pass to the northern side and head north-west towards a nearby band of rocks. Go through them and then follow a line of waymarks down into a stony valley embraced by rough cliffs and crags. On the left-hand side of this valley the descent leads to a landscape of grassy hummocks. Pass through a fold between two such hummocks and descend quite steeply beyond, winding down the hillside with plenty of waymarks to guide you across a broad open grassland, making towards the huts of Ober Stafel seen ahead.

At the second building (1746m) bear left, then descend in a series of zig-zags over rough pastureland, and in about 10 minutes from the alp join the path used on the upward route. Descend to Unter Stafel and then follow the winding road down to the valley. One of the reasons for doing so is to have the opportunity to study at close hand a rather fine waterfall whose stream is crossed by the road just below.

Route 31:	Bisistal (Sahli; 1149m) - Firner Loch (2248m)- Urnerboden (1372m)
Grade:	3
Distance:	8 kilometres
Height gain:	1099 metres
Height loss:	876 metres
Time:	4-4½ hours
Map:	L.S. 246 Klausenpass 1:50,000

The crossing of the Firner Loch is one of the classic pass routes in this corner of the mountains. It is achieved either directly from Sahli in the Bisistal proper, or from the Glattalp Hut, both paths meeting at the pass. The following brief outline is given for the direct route.

Begin as for Route 30 by crossing the bridge over the stream at the road-head near the cable-car station, and walk up the winding farm road. Where it forks continue ahead, then break away to the left on a line of waymarks leading steeply uphill to the left of a stream. On coming to a wooden bridge cross the stream and continue uphill, still following waymarks which lead to a crossing track.

Go over the track and climb on, still following waymarks. Eventually these will bring you to Gwalpeten, a cluster of alp huts at 1522 metres. Above to the left rises the Marenspitz (2280m), ahead the ridge curves south-westward. South of the alp the route rises gradually, then swings eastward to climb steeply into a rocky corner of the mountains. In this rocky corner you come to the Firner Loch (2248m) on the borders of canton Schwyz and canton Uri. The descent to the south-east is stony at first, but it becomes more green and promising lower down towards the alp of Firnen (1875m). Below this you descend a line of cliffs to another small alp (Hüfi; 1713), from which the way drops over steep grass slopes to the Klausenpass road a short stroll upvalley from Urnerboden.

Urnerboden has hotel and *Matratzenlager* accommodation; Postbus links with Linthal, Klausenpass and Altdorf.

Route 32:	Bisistal (Sahli; 1149m) - Glattalp Hut (1896m)
Grade:	3
Distance:	5 kilometres
Height gain:	747 metres
Time:	2 hours
Map:	L.S. 246 Klausenpass 1:50,000

Owned by the Mythen Section of the SAC the Glattalp Hut stands in a landscape of grass and large bands of limestone, a haunting countryside when mists are writhing, but bright and cheery under a warm sun and spoilt only by the pylons of the Sahli-Glattalp cableway. To the north-east, but out of sight, is the Glattalpsee, and above and beyond the lake rise the Höch Turm (2666m), Ortstock (2727m) and the long wall of the Jegerstöck. The hut serves as a useful base for the exploration of much interesting country, and a glance at the map will give an idea of the wealth of opportunities available. If you plan to stay for several days at the hut and are heavily laden, it would doubtless be preferable to ride the cable-car from Sahli and walk the short distance necessary in about 30 minutes. This approach walk, however, is worth tackling for itself - whether or not you plan to stay overnight. It's a steep and strenuous walk, but taken at a leisurely pace you'll find much to enjoy on the way. (Note that there is not always a guardian on duty, so you may need to take your own food if you plan to stay.)

Cross the bridge over the Muota River just north of the Sahli-Glattalp cable-car station, and follow the farm road as it winds uphill. There is a fine view off to the right to a superb waterfall cascading through the woods opposite. When the road forks after about 10 to 15 minutes bear left, climbing still towards Glattalp and Milchbüelen. About 5 minutes later break away on a clear waymarked path which goes straight ahead when the road veers left. (Painted on a rock at the start of the path are the letters SAC and Glattalp.) This path takes you up a series of timber-reinforced steps to reach a sloping pastureland, which it skirts along the right-hand edge. At the eastern end of the pasture the path can be seen making a rising traverse of the headwall above which Glattalp will be found - though not seen until you reach it.

Halfway along this traverse path an alternative route is offered. A more narrow path, also *Bergweg* waymarked, slants up to the right; it's narrow, steep and somewhat exposed in places, and it acts as a short-cut while the main trail winds round on a more gentle incline. The two paths merge again a little higher. Before long the way eases for a brief spell alongside a stream with a fine example of limestone pavement on the left, and just beyond this is a small tarn.

Above the tarn the path forks again. The right-hand trail goes to the Glattalpsee by way of the Glattalp restaurant (near the cable-car terminus), and is marked to Ortstock, while the left-hand option leads to the Glattalp Hut. Just above the path divide you can see the hut ahead. It is reached in about 15 minutes from here, after passing another section of limestone pavement.

Route 33:	Glattalp Hut (1896m) - Furggele (2395m)

Grade:	3
Distance:	7 kilometres
Height gain:	499 metres
Height loss:	52 metres
Time:	2-2½ hours
Map:	L.S. 246 Klausenpass 1:50,000

From the Glattalp Hut there are two walking routes across the mountains to the traffic-free resort of Braunwald above the Linth valley in canton Glarus. One is by way of the Erigsmatt (2082m) at the head of the Charetalp, north of the hut; the other is via the pass of Furggele in the ridge linking the Höch Turm and Ortstock. This last, however, should not be attempted by hill-walkers inexperienced in snow and ice work, for on the eastern side of the pass there is an extremely steep descent to begin with, and this crosses a series of small glaciers and snowfields. (During the research for this guide the pass was found to be heavily corniced and impassable even in midsummer.) On the approach to the pass from Glattalp it is also possible that there will be steep snowslopes to contend with. But you should be able to assess the situation long before you get to it. Caution is advised.

Furggele is an obvious long, narrow saddle between the sharp tower of the Höch Turm (seen to the left) and the easy lump of the Ortstock, the ascent of which is usually made by way of the pass from where there is something of a path.

From the hut descend by a clear trail into the bed of the Glattalp and walk across to the cable-car terminus with its restaurant nearby. Beyond the cable-car station descend a little on a waymarked track. When it forks bear left with waymarks to guide you. The lake of the Glattalpsee is now seen ahead and the track, then path, heads above the left-hand shoreline with the walls of the Jegerstöck on the far side suggesting much rock climbing potential.

As the trail veers to the right at the far end of the lake, go straight ahead following a line of waymarks upvalley (there are also waymarks heading right to confuse). A path reappears keeping to the left of the main valley stream which feeds the lake. The path soon begins to climb, crosses the stream and heads among screes and rocky terraces. The saddle of Furggele is always prominent above, so should there be snowslopes obscuring the path it will be obvious where to aim for. But take caution if so.

The pass is reached in about $2^{1}/2$ hours from the hut (depending on conditions). From it you can gaze down steep plunging slopes to green meadows above Braunwald. To the left the Höch Turm looks fine, while gazing back the way you have come the dazzle of sun in the Glattalpsee catches the eye. Descend by the same route, taking particular care on the upper slopes.

Other Walks in the Bisistal:

An extension of Route 33 above is suggested on the *Muotatal Wanderkarte*. It crosses the **FURGGELE** pass and descends nearly 400m on the eastern side. (Caution advised - see above.) The route then makes a rising traverse of the slopes below Höch Turm and Flätstock to **ERIGSMATT**, followed by a descent through the **CHARETALP** back to the **GLATTALP HUT**. This grade 3 route would take around 7 hours to complete.

Another circular route from the **GLATTALP HUT** (or from Sahli) heads south and climbs to the **FIRNER LOCH** (the pass crossed in Route 31). But instead of crossing the pass, descend north-westwards from it to the alp of **GWALPETEN** and down towards the valley, before striking uphill again on the hut approach path described under Route 32. This is another grade 3 route, taking about $6^{1}/2$ hours.

Also worth considering, should you plan to leave the area for valleys farther south, is to cross the **BALMER GRÄTLI** (visited on Route 30) direct from the valley via **OBER STAFEL**, and descend on the far side to the **KLAUSENPASS**.

Strong and experienced mountain walkers could also create a multi-day circuit over the mountains above the Glattalp Hut to the Linth and Urnerboden valleys. Either cross the **ERIGSMATT** or **FURGGELE** and descend to **BRAUNWALD** (day 1). Then have an easy day's walk on a belvedere path to **URNERBODEN** (day 2), and return to the **BISISTAL** either across the **FIRNER LOCH** or up to the Klausenpass and over the **BALMER GRÄTLI** (day 3).

Accommodation is available at the end of each stage.

Another full day's walk which crosses to the Schächental well below the Klausenpass, is a 7-hour cross-country challenge that initially heads north-west out of **SCHWARZENBACH**, then cuts back southward to gain the hillside at **GALTENABNET**, passing the alp of **HÜTTENBODEN**. The saddle of **GANDER FUR** (2016m) is crossed in the south-eastern wall of the Hürital. Continue to **RINDERMATT** (1818m) then climb to the **CHINZIG CHULM** (see Hürital section below) and descend to **BIEL** for a cable-car link with the lower **SCHÄCHENTAL**. A grade 3 route.

For further ideas, study the *Muotatal Wanderkarte* (scale 1:25,000) on sale from various shops and tourist information offices in the area.

HÜRITAL

A shorter valley than the neighbouring Bisistal, the Hürital is nonetheless another delightful alpine backwater served by a minor road (no buses) heading south from Hinterthal. This too is headed by grey limestone peaks whose southern barrier wall is breached by a couple of foot passes that lead to the Schächental. Subdividing the upper reaches of the valley is the curving Chinzerberg (2138m) that projects directly from the main ridge barrier. North of the Chinzerberg is the high pastureland of Seenalp, which is also walled by the Chaiserstock (among others), while to the south and east is the steeply sloping Chinzertal. On the eastern side of the valley opposite the Chinzertal is another high grassland known as Matten, above which an easy pass takes a trail over to the Bisistal.

The drive up into the Hürital from the main Muotatal is splendid. First winding through steep meadows, then into forest and finally opening to the gentle nature of the valley, a blend of pasture, patches of forest and neat-looking mountains. Parking is to be had with discretion beside the road. (Be careful not to block the road, and be warned that cattle often graze alongside it.) Refreshment and limited accommodation is possible at the valley's only hamlet of Liplisbüel.

Route 34:	Hinterthal (624m) - Liplisbüel (1194m)

Grade:	1-2
Distance:	4 kilometres
Height gain:	570 metres
Time:	2 hours
Map:	L.S. 246 Klausenpass 1:50,000

This pleasant and mostly easy valley walk is offered for those without their own transport. Buses run from Schwyz into the Muotatal. Alight in Hinterthal and walk upvalley along the road a short distance. When the road bears left to cross the river continue ahead and a few paces later turn right by a restaurant. The Hürital road now begins to climb the hillside ahead. At the first bend a footpath short-cut heads uphill, crosses the road a little later and follows along the left-hand side of the Hüribach, soon among trees and gaining height all the way. Entering the Hürital proper the path follows the road on the eastern side of the river heading south and climbing to Liplisbüel, a charming huddle of dark, shingle-walled chalets on the left of the road and with a small tarn nearby.

Route 35:	Liplisbüel (1194m) - Seenalper Seeli (1719m)

Grade:	2-3
Distance:	4 kilometres
Height gain:	525 metres
Time:	2 hours
Map:	L.S. 246 Klausenpass 1:50,000

A short walk, but steep in places, it leads to a lake hidden in a rucked pastureland below some fine-looking mountains. On the slopes leading to the lake early summer splashes colour with alpenroses in great clusters, while many other cushion plants adorn boulders and grassy hummocks around the lake.

From Liplisbüel walk upvalley along the road until it crosses a bridge to the left-hand side of the stream. Leave the road here and follow along the right-hand side (west bank) on a vague path. About 15 minutes after leaving the road you will come to a faint junction of paths with a signpost directing you to the right to Seenalp and Chinzig Chulm. The path is not altogether clear, but there are a few waymarks guiding up the side of a conifer woodland to the left of a stream. The way becomes more clear as you gain height.

About 45 minutes from Liplisbüel you come onto a farm road and bear right. This will lead you up to the alp building of Seenalp (1515m). (It is possible to short-cut the road by taking a direct path straight up to the alp.)

Opposite the building a path (waymarked) heads steeply up a nose of hillside bright with alpenroses in early summer. Above this spur the way crosses a ruffled pastureland with steep rock walls rising on the right above long slopes of scree, reminiscent of the Dolomites.

Approximately 45 minutes from the alp building you will notice the Seenalper Seeli tarn lying below on the left, cupped in a grassy basin. It makes a good place for a picnic. Wander round the lake (it has no outlet stream) to extend your views before descending to the valley by the same route. (Allow about 1¹/₂ hours for the return to Liplisbüel.)

Route 36:	Liplisbüel (1194m) - Chinzig Chulm (2073m) - Alp Chinzertal (1847m) - Liplisbüel

Grade:	3
Distance:	17 kilometres
Height gain/loss:	879 metres
Time:	6-6¹/₂ hours
Map:	L.S. 246 Klausenpass 1:50,000

A full day's commitment is demanded for this walk, but it promises much and those promises will be fulfilled. There are grassy alps, a small tarn, extensive views, a fine historic pass, a dramatic waterfall and graceful mountains as a constant backdrop. It is rather an energetic circuit (often tackled in the reverse direction), but a popular one with those Swiss who have discovered it.

Follow directions as for Route 35 as far as the Seenalper Seeli (1719m; 2 hours) and continue beyond it on a steadily rising path. Above the tarn there are patches of limestone pavement and plenty of alpine plants. The trail is clear and waymarked, and it leads over grass slopes and several minor streams, and as you gain height towards the head of the valley you will see a small hut perched on what appears from below to be a grassy saddle. The path swings left (south) below the hut and passes through a region of limestone pits and grass bowls. Snow sometimes lingers here late into the summer.

It's an undulating trail until you emerge through a narrow cleft and descend into a limestone-scarred region. Come to a junction of tracks (one path breaks away to the right to wander along the southern side of a grass ridge to cross it at Früttstagen; 1918m). Ignore this right-hand path, continue ahead and, about 15 minutes from the first hut, you will see a second hut just below, unmarked on the 1:50,000 map. Do not go down to this hut but take the upper of two paths which climbs towards a large cross and brings you to the pass of Chinzig Chulm (about 3 hours 45 mins from Liplisbüel).

This pass is a splendid site: grassy on one side, dramatically rocky on the other, with limestone clefts and crags falling from the ridge. It is marked by a shrine and a signpost. Views are fine in all directions and include distant snowpeaks with small glaciers, Dolomite-like rock peaks, blue-hinted valleys and sloping pastures.

To return to the Hürital go to the right of the cross and take the descending path in the direction of Alp Chinzertal. About ten minutes from the pass the trail forks. (The right-hand option goes to Rindermatt and the Bisistal - a long but rewarding cross-country journey.) Take the left-hand trail, continuing the descent to reach the rather untidy Alp Chinzertal (1847m; 4 hours 15 mins) slumped in the midst of a mass of dock, snug below the southern crags of the Chinzerberg. Pass through the alp and continue to descend, crossing one or two streams and joining a farm track. This leads all the way to the main valley, but can be short-cut in places by footpaths. As you wind round the

Oberalpstock from the path to the Windgällen Hut (Route 52)

The pass of Chinzig-Chulm at the head of the Hürital (Routes 36-38)
The high path at Nideralp above the Schächental (Route 42)

hillside along the track, so you have lovely views up to the jagged peaks that form the dividing wall between the upper Hürital and the Bisistal; a splendid waterfall sprays below them.

In Wangi, the upper valley, the track takes you past several farm buildings, and at Point 1429m, as you come to more buildings, waymarks indicate an alternative way off to the right. Descend to the stream and cross a bridge to the right bank, and follow the path leading down across pastures. This leads to another track that eventually feeds onto the main Hürital road which you follow as far as Liplisbüel.

Route 37:	Liplisbüel (1194m) - Chinzig Chulm (2073m) - Biel (1637m)
Grade:	3
Distance:	10 kilometres
Height gain:	879 metres
Height loss:	436 metres
Time:	4¹/₂-5 hours
Map:	L.S. 246 Klausenpass 1:50,000

The crossing of Chinzig Chulm between the Muotatal (Hürital) and the Schächental is one of the classic pass routes of Central Switzerland and, as has already been noted, is one of those traversed by Suvorov and his forces in 1799.

Follow directions for Route 36 from Liplisbüel to the pass (3 hours 45 mins). Crossing through bear right on the waymarked trail that swings round the head of a steep corrie, then descend to the cable-car station of Biel (about one hour from the pass). Refreshments and accommodation (beds and *Matratzenlager*) are both available here. The cableway connects this upper hillside with Brugg near Burglen in the Schächental almost 1000 metres below.

Note: Purists might wish to ignore the cable-car and walk all the way. In that case it might be more enjoyable (and less-punishing on the knees) to make a steady westward traverse of the hillside to Eggberge and either descend from there to Flüelen or to Altdorf. The high trail is joined at Point 1720m (above the Biel cable-car station) where you bear right and follow it all the way to Eggberge (1445m; 2 hours 45 mins from Point 1720m). There you will find gasthaus accommodation, and from Eggberge the town of Flüelen is a little over two hours away; Altdorf is about the same. Total walking time: Liplizbüel to Altdorf/Flüelen, about 9^{1}/$_{2}$ hours.

Route 38:	Liplisbüel (1194m) - Chinzig Chulm (2073m) - Ratzi (1511m)
Grade:	3
Distance:	12 kilometres
Height gain:	879 metres
Height loss:	562 metres
Time:	4^{1}/$_{2}$-5 hours
Map:	L.S. 246 Klausenpass 1:50,000

This is a variation of Route 37 and is a useful option for those walkers intending to move on to an exploration of the Schächental and the Klausenpass area.

The route to the Chinzig Chulm is the same as that described for Route 36, but instead of descending by the right-hand trail on the southern side of the pass, take the left-hand option heading almost due south and sloping down the hillside for about 1 hour 10 minutes in order to gain the cable-car station of Ratzi, which is linked with Spiringen in the valley.

Other Walks in the Hurital:
Those routes described above all project towards the head of the valley. There are others, of course, one of which heads east across the walling mountains and descends into the Bisistal. This 4^{1}/$_{2}$-hour walk (grade 3) begins just south of **LIPLISBÜEL** where the road crosses to the right bank of the stream. A path climbs up the eastern hillside to **OBEREN TRASMEREN** (1986m) and skirts below the cliffs of **WASSERBERGFIRST**, descending to **GIGEN** then mostly through

forest to **SCHWARZENBACH** in the **BISISTAL**.

Study the map for further ideas.

PRAGEL PASS REGION

The Pragel Pass (1550m) may not constitute one of the great mountain crossings of the Alps, but it has undisputed charm. It's a low-slung saddle of pasture between the Mieserenstock (2199m) and the broad mass of the Silberen, a pleasant, sunny place across which an undramatic road links the cantons of Schwyz and Glarus. The pass is not served by public transport (although Postbuses journey from Glarus to the hamlet of Richisau (1132m) on the north-eastern side), and the road beyond the pass is closed to motor traffic at weekends. Up there the sound of cowbells does not have to compete with the Postbus horn. Soft, and in places spongy, meadows sweep below the long rock walls that mark the northern limits of the valley leading to it, while the lower reaches of that valley, the valley of the Starzlen stream, are heavily clothed with forest. The Starzlen drains into the Muota at Hinterthal where a path begins its climb towards the pass.

There are no villages in the valley of the Starzlen, but there are plenty of alp farms to exploit the rich grasslands. In the meadows of the Berglen Alp, especially near the stream, local Swiss families gather for picnics on summer weekends, while just short of the pass there is a restaurant beside the road.

Although the valley leading to the pass is somewhat limited in its range of walking opportunities, it is recommended for at least one day's visit, and the route offered below, though short, will help express some of the charms of the area.

Route 39:	Fruttli (1220m) - Bergen Alp - Pragel Pass (1550m)
Grade:	1
Distance:	4 kilometres
Height gain:	330 metres
Time:	1½ hours
Maps:	L.S. 246 Klausenpass and 236 Lachen 1:50,000

For walkers with their own transport the following itinerary will make an enjoyable morning's walk. (Should you have no transport of your own the lower section of the path begins on the north side of the Muota in Hinterthal, and remains on the west flank of the Starzlen's valley as far as Fruttli. Add approximately 1½ hours to the walk.)

Drive up the Pragel road from Hinterthal for about 5 kilometres. The road then makes a sharp right-hand bend, but on the left of the road a dirt track breaks away among trees. This is Fruttli. At the entrance to the track there is a footpath signpost and sufficient room to park a few cars with care.

Walk along the track heading roughly eastward above the stream. The way is mostly shaded by trees and rises slightly to bring you in about 15 minutes to the lower reaches of Berglen Alp. On the right of the track stands the timber-built Pragelblick Hut. Now the track crosses the stream and strikes off across pastureland with a few alp buildings in it. At the eastern end of the pasture the track forks. Take the left branch, in effect continuing ahead, and now rising as a path uphill.

Passing a wooden shelter you come to a large cross beside the path, and enter an upper pasture with a number of small streams draining through. Without diverting from the main trail you will come directly to the alp of Pragel itself; the road snakes in from the right, a chapel and restaurant beside the road. In 1½ hours from Fruttli you arrive at the pass.

Other Walks from the Pragel Pass:
To walk all the way from **HINTERTHAL** to **RICHISAU** on the eastern side (a popular crossing) will take about 5-5½ hours, grade 1-2. From Richisau you can take the Postbus to Glarus and return to Schwyz by a roundabout train journey.

Walkers who go up to the Pragel Pass by car and park there can tackle a circular walk of the **SILBEREN** (5 hours, grade 3; good conditions essential).

An interesting crossing of the mountains to the **WAGITAL** is another recommended outing from the Pragel Pass. It entails following a trail which starts just below the pass on the Glarus side. This trail rises to cross a spur at 1617m below the Fläschenspitz, then through
100

a minor pass at 1573m followed by a descent to the **WAGITALER SEE**. This crossing will take about 4 hours (grade 3). At the far end of the Wagital lake there's a Postbus service down to Wangen near the Lake of Zürich.

Elsewhere in the Muotatal:
The pick of the Muotatal's walking routes are to be found in the feeder valleys, but there are several routes in and around the main valley that deserve to be mentioned. One follows the left bank of the river for much of the way through the valley from **MUOTATHAL** and after emerging at its lower end, swings off to **SCHWYZ**. This undemanding, yet enjoyable grade 1 walk will take about two hours.

The sunny, traffic-free resort of **STOOS** (visited on Route 8 from Brunnen) is accessible by funicular from Schlattli at the western end of the valley. There are several good walks from there, one of which winds along the hillsides that form the southern wall of the Muotatal, and comes down to **HINTERTHAL**, a walk of about $4^{1}/_{2}$ hours (grade 3).

A link with the **URNERSEE** is possible from the Muotatal. From the PTT in **MUOTATHAL** village head south-west, wind up the wooded hillside to **RIEDMATTLI**, then climb steadily to the pass of **HÖCHI** (1487m). West of this you descend into the Riemenstaldner Tal and, about $4^{1}/_{2}$ hours from Muotathal, come to **RIEMENSTALDEN** (1030m). This little village has a Postbus service down to Sisikon on the lakeside. Otherwise the walk will require an additional $1^{1}/_{2}$ hours (6 hours in all). A fine walk, grade 3.

KLAUSENPASS REGION

Position:	**South-east of the Urnersee, and comprising the valleys of Schächental, Brunnital and Urnerboden in cantons Uri and Glarus.**
Map:	**L.S. 246 Klausenpass 1:50,000**
Bases:	**Altdorf (454m), Burglen (559m), Unterschächen (995m), Urnerboden (1372m)**
Tourist Information:	**Verkehrsbüro, 6460 Altdorf (Tel: 044 2 2888)**
	Informationsstelle, Dorfplatz, 6463 Burglen (Tel: 044 2 2643)
	Postbüro, 8751 Urnerboden (Tel: 058 84 1705)

The Klausenpass (1948m) is one of the most attractive and scenic of alpine crossings. Unlike some higher, better-known passes this is not a bleak, monochrome saddle littered with dirty snow throughout the summer. Instead it's an often flower-speckled place of sunshine and far views overlooked by the strange lump of the Marcherstöckli to the north and a thrusting spur of Clariden to the south. Below the pass to the east lies the beautiful U-shaped valley of Urnerboden, to the west the more steeply-set wedge of the Schächental. Each has its own special appeal, its own set of individual features that reward all who go wandering there.

The long northern wall of peaks that runs virtually undisturbed from the shores of the Urnersee (the southern arm of the Vierwaldstättersee) to the Ortstock, a distance of nearly 35 kilometres, forms the boundary of both the Schächental and valley of Urnerboden. North of that wall lie tributary valleys of the Muotatal, while at its eastern limit the Linth Tal makes a lengthy ditch running roughly south to north from the Tödi's glaciers to Glarus and beyond, its waters eventually draining into the Lake of Zürich.

Along the southern wall of the Schächental the mountains are more confused and less regular in their alignment. Their western extent is a curious moulding of spurs and ridges and tight

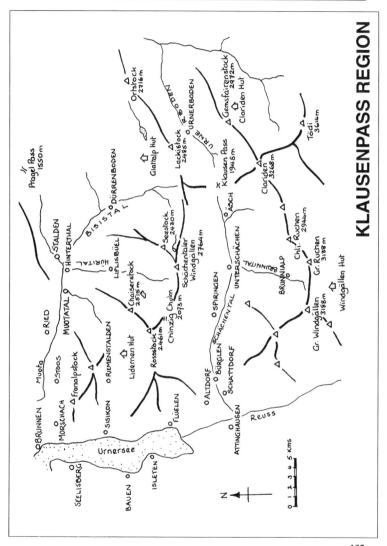

KLAUSENPASS REGION

amphitheatres. Minor glens drain out of them in an arc, into either the Reuss valley or the lower Schächental itself until, that is, you come to the more formal Brunnital, a glen of exquisite loveliness that runs northward from the vast faces of the Windgällen and Ruchen peaks to join the Schächental proper at Unterschächen. East of the Brunnital the mountains make an attempt to conform, and by the time they've reached their apex on the summit of the Clariden (3268m) they've created unity of purpose, and the extending ridge that includes the Gemsfairenstock makes an orderly southern wall for the Urnerboden valley, a ridge that subsides gently to forest.

On either side of the Klausenpass the nature of the two valleys is quite different. For all its gentle breadth and flat-bottomed ease one would suspect the valley of Urnerboden to have been developed by village communities of some size. It looks as though it could produce prosperity; at least one major resort might be expected there. But this has not happened. Instead it's a delightful, unchanging high pastoral plateau and its tiny hamlets exist around the summer grazing of cattle. There's only one village (and that barely more than a hamlet) known as Urnerboden, the same as the valley, and despite its several hotels it could not be classed as a resort; a fine base for walking holidays though. The Schächental, on the other hand, supports a handful of villages that appear to have been terraced out of the steeply-plunging hillsides. High above them those same slopes are peppered with chalets and haybarns, with tracks and narrow farm roads that climb in tortuous windings to lonely alp hamlets whose windows gaze south at a wonderland of mountains. Downvalley from Unterschächen a few cableways lace the slopes, but the villages that promote them show only limited development and, in common with Urnerboden, could hardly be called resorts. Quiet villages, they are, with some acommodation. No show, no glitz, just a village atmosphere and the simple pleasures of wandering high mountain trails as their sole attraction. Does anyone need more for a walking holiday?

The pass is generally open from about late April until November, but precise dates, of course, vary from year to year and depend on the period and depth of snowfall. A Postbus service operates across the

Klausenpass between Flüelen and Linthal (service 600.30) from late June to late October. To check details enquire at one of the tourist information offices, or by telephone: 044 2 2185.

Main Valley Bases:

ALTDORF (454m) is actually situated in the Reuss valley just south of the Urnersee, but below the mouth of the Schächental. From it the Klausenpass road snakes eastward to Burglen and beyond. Altdorf, therefore, makes a reasonable base for those who wish to explore countryside farther east, as well as the riches of the Urnersee and other glens accessible from the Reuss valley. It's the capital of canton Uri, a town of some 8200 inhabitants, a centre for the William Tell cult focussed on a large bronze statue in the *Rathausplatz*, and the summer production of Schiller's well-known play which helps keep the legend alive. Altdorf has a number of attractive buildings and a small-town atmosphere. It has modern shopping facilities, banks, restaurants, PTT, and several hotels.

BURGLEN (559m) is the first village community on the Klausenpass road, reached about 3 kilometres from Altdorf, and is picturesquely built on a hillock around which the hairpins of the road twist uncomfortably. It is said to have been William Tell's birthplace, and on the site of his house stands a chapel (built 1582) that has been highly decorated with scenes of his exploits. Nearby, in the old tower of the Wattigwiler, is a Tell Museum. Burglen also has a Tell monument dating from 1786 and a seventeenth-century Baroque parish church. In the village there are one or two restaurants; a choice of accommodation (including *Matratzenlager*) is available in hotels and gasthofs. At Brugg, upvalley a short distance, a cable-car rises via Rietlig to Biel below the Chinzig Chulm pass.

UNTERSCHÄCHEN (995m) lies at the entrance to the Brunnital, a little over halfway through the Schächental and about 12 kilometres short of the Klausenpass. There are some splendid walks to be had directly from the village whose setting is its most charming feature. There are a few shops and restaurants and a small amount of hotel accommodation.

URNERBODEN (1372m) on the eastern side of the Klausenpass is a small collection of buildings gathered alongside the road and round a square below the church to the south of it. (Lovely views up to the snows of Clariden.) It has a post office, one general store and several modest hotels and *gasthofs*, some of which offer *Matratzenlager* accommodation. A good base from which to spend a few days walking, the peace and tranquillity of the village is broken only by the clatter of cowbells and the tuneful horn of the Postbus echoing along the valley.

Other Accommodation:

On the northern slopes of the Schächental overnight accommodation is offered in a number of fairly remote, but scenic places. **EGGBERGE** is one *(Gasthaus)*. This is reached by cable-car from Flüelen, or by a 3-hour walk from Altdorf (see Route 11). **BIEL** (1634m) is another. Reached by cable-car from Brugg near Burglen, it nestles below the Chinzig Chulm and offers lodging in both bedrooms and *Matratzenlager*.

In the valley near Altdorf, **SCHATTDORF** has hotel accommodation on the southern edge of the entrance to the Schächental. Upvalley both **BRUGG** and **SPIRINGEN** have a limited number of beds, as does the beautifully-situated roadside hamlet of **URIGEN** just west of the Klausenpass, while there's also a hotel at the **KLAUSENPASS** itself. Accessible from Urnerboden is the traffic-free resort village of **BRAUNWALD**, set upon a shelf of hillside above Linthal (there is a high path round this shelf from Urnerboden). Braunwald has a youth hostel (90 beds) and several hotels.

Mountain Huts:

The only SAC hut accessible to walkers from the Klausenpass region is the **CLARIDEN HUT** (2453m). Reached by a walk of 4-5 hours from Urnerboden, this 84-bed hut is located to the south-west of the Gemsfairenstock. Owned by the Bachtel Section meals are available when the guardian is in residence, which is mainly in mid-summer. The telephone number for bookings is 058 84 3121.

THE SCHÄCHENTAL

Leaving the Reuss valley and the main Gotthard route immediately to the south of Altdorf, the Klausenpass road breaks away to the east and climbs into the lower reaches of the Schächental at Burglen. At once it becomes obvious that this valley is of a very different nature from that of the Reuss. It's a steep-sided V-shaped valley, green and bright and full of promise. (The Reuss is often dark and gloomy with heavy shadow and the mystery of stark-walled gorges.) East of Burglen, near the Brugg-Biel cable-car station, the road crosses to the north bank of the Schächen stream and remains there all the way to the pass, climbing but little until some sharp hairpin bends bring it to the village of Spiringen (923m).

The river is now deep below while the road runs along the hillside on a natural terrace at a regular contour all the way to Unterschächen, by which time the valley bed has risen almost to road-level. At Unterschächen all eyes turn to the right, drawn by the hinted beauty of the Brunnital with its great rock walls enclosing the southern end in an impressive amphitheatre.

Outside Unterschächen the road twists and turns and slants up to Urigen (1276m) and, rising still, passes through short galleries in the rock below the Schächentaler Windgällen. From the road here it is possible to look down onto the fabulous Stauben Falls cascading in phantoms of spray above the hamlet of Äsch some 300 metres below the road (better seen from a footpath leading into the hamlet). On a comfortable contour the road continues heading east along the steep hillside, writhes once again with hairpins near Unter Balm and shortly after emerges through a brief moorland-like region onto the Klausenpass proper.

So much for the road. On both north and south flanks of the mountains high trails connect summer-only alp farms and, especially on the northern side, walkers' passes cross the walling mountains at altitudes of more than 2000 metres. Down in the valley bed too there are farm trails picked out regularly through the centuries by men and women going about their daily business.

This, then, is a walker's landscape. The following few routes will give a taste of the region and, hopefully, lead you to discover more for yourself.

Route 40:	Klausenpass (1948m) - Heidmanegg (1862m) - Eggberge (1447m) - Altdorf (454m)

Grade:	**2-3**
Distance:	**26 kilometres**
Height loss:	**1494 metres**
Time:	**9 hours (or 2 days)**
Map:	**L.S. 246 Klausenpass 1:50,000**

By linking a series of footpaths, trails and farm roads, this splendid *Höhenweg* (high route) has been created to run the length of the Schächental. As it traces the upper northern slopes of the valley it's a sun-catching walk. Views to the south, and into the depths of the Schächental, are stunning, and there's constant interest along the way with a variety of alp huts and chalets and tiny summer-only hamlets to pass through. Should you decide to cut short the walk and descend to the valley there are many steep, knee-jarring trails to choose from, but in addition there are cableways too in a few places. And in order to break the walk into a two-day journey, accommodation is available at Biel, a few minutes' walk below Point 1720m, some four hours after leaving the Klausenpass, and also at Eggberge before the final descent to Altdorf begins.

Just south of the little chapel at the Klausenpass a footpath signpost directs a narrow path to Unter Balm and Äsch. Follow this as it descends a little below the road and follows its general direction for about thirty minutes. The trail then comes onto the road (near Unter Balm) and crosses to a track cutting away from the hairpin a few paces up the road. This track contours along the hillside heading west and comes to the hamlet of Heidmanegg (1862m; 1 hour 15 mins).

The continuing route leads to Hegen, Tristel, Rietlig and on to Unter Gisleralp (1685m) below the Chinzig Chulm in about 3½ hours. Approximately half an hour later you come to the trail junction at Point 1720m. Immediately below is the Biel cable-car station with prospects of refreshment and overnight accommodation. A steep path descends to it.

Heading west still the high trail curves round the head of more corries, comes to the tarn of Flesch (1812m) in a little under two hours from Point 1720m, and on a descending path leads to Eggberge in another hour. This panoramic viewpoint also has refreshments and accommodation, as well as a cable-car link with Flüelen on the edge of the Urnersee. A forest track takes you down to Altdorf from here in about 2 hours 15 minutes.

Route 41:	Klausenpass (1948m) - Äsch (1234m) - Unterschächen (995m)

Grade:	**2**
Distance:	**7 kilometres**
Height loss:	**953 metres**
Time:	**2¹/₂-3 hours**
Map:	**L.S. 246 Klausenpass 1:50,000**

Although this is a comparatively short walk it is worth giving a full day to it. Should you be staying in Unterschächen, for example, you could take a morning Postbus to the Klausenpass, descend as far as the hamlet of Äsch and spend time in the meadows there, enjoying the glorious sight of the huge Stauben Falls pouring from a cleft of the mountain above. Laze by the river and eat a picnic lunch, listen to the music of insects in the meadows, study the wild flowers or simply absorb the gentle beauty of the valley. Then amble slowly down the dirt road towards Unterschächen.

This particular walk forms a small part of the classic long-distance trek, the Alpine Pass Route (Sargans to Montreux).

Beginning near the chapel at the Klausenpass the start is identical to Route 40. A footpath signpost indicates a trail heading downhill below the road in the direction of Unter Balm and Äsch. The trail is rather marshy at first and it leads in a slightly descending traverse just below the level of the road. In places the path fades, but you continue in the same general direction as the road and after about 30 minutes come to it again at a hairpin bend. Do not go onto the road,

The lovely hamlet of Äsch in the Schächental

however, but cut back a few paces and cross a stream, then veer right (south-east) on a grassy path which crosses another stream (the Vorder Schächen) near the farm buildings of Unter Balm. Pass to the right of these and follow a waymarked path which swings through a gap and begins a steep zig-zag descent below a line of cliffs.

After a section of handrails has finished, and near the bottom of the zig-zags, keep alert for an insignificant-looking trail which branches off to the right. There are no signs or waymarks that this is the path to Äsch, but it is important not to miss it. It descends quite steeply with views of the Schächental stretching ahead enticingly and, as you descend towards it, the hamlet of Äsch comes into view.

Easy undulating meadows bring you into Äsch with its huge waterfall seen off to the left. Walk through the hamlet (it's in two parts) and follow the dirt road beyond, signposted to Unterschächen. The track passes through a woodyard and comes onto the road at Ribi, but you break away to the left a few paces later, and descend on a path which takes you past several farms and through pastures and brings you directly to Unterschächen.

Route 42:	Unterschächen (995m) - Äsch (1234m) - Nideralp (1652m) - Trogenalp (1500m) - Brunnialp (1402m) - Unterschächen

Grade:	3
Distance:	16 kilometres
Height gain/loss:	657 metres
Time:	6½-7 hours
Map:	L.S. 246 Klausenpass 1:50,000

An energetic day's walking is to be had along this circuit, but there are so many lovely features to enjoy that any weariness will be well repaid. One of the highlights is the hamlet of Äsch with its waterfall, but after you've had an opportunity to study that from below, the route then climbs steeply up the mountainside to cross above it (though it has to be said, the waterfall is not actually seen from above). There follows a delightful high belvedere of a trail round the hillside from one isolated alp to another, before curving into the Brunnital with wonderful views of the Gross Windgällen. The descent through the Brunnital to Unterschächen underlines its charm.

The walk begins in the main street of Unterschächen, and heads up the Klausenpass road for a short distance until you're almost clear of the village. A track leads off to the right, signposted to Äsch. This takes you past some houses and between meadows heading east. When you come onto the road again at Ribi (1055m) walk a few paces to another minor road which descends to the right and goes through a woodyard. Beyond this cross the Vorder Schächen stream and walk alongside it on the dirt track to Äsch, the second part of which is noted for its beautiful waterfall.

Continue walking upvalley beyond the hamlet on a waymarked path heading towards the Klausenpass. This soon begins to climb quite steeply up rucked slopes with a choice of waterfalls spraying down to right and left. About thirty minutes beyond Äsch you will come to a rock on the path with the following destinations painted on it: Klausen (to the left) and Oberalp (to the right). Just before you reach this rock (1375m) desert the main trail and follow the right-hand path. It is more narrow than the Klausenpass route, but is still adequately waymarked. It zig-zags up among trees with cascades off to the right.

Above the trees you emerge to a delightful bowl of meadowland with streams flowing through, and come to another trail junction. Continue ahead to the right, in the direction of Nideralp, Wannelen and Oberalp. The way now rises quite steeply again to emerge in a high rough meadowland pitted here and there with rocks and with a waterfall spraying down ahead which eventually becomes (out of sight) the Stauben Falls which give Äsch its character. The path crosses the stream and just beyond the bridge comes to another junction of paths. Continue straight ahead to Nideralp (in 45 minutes). (The left-hand path climbs to Oberalp and the Klausenpass.)

The way rises and falls among alder scrub and then comes into the open with Nideralp seen ahead. It is a small, rather untidy alp of two buildings; from it a track leads on a nearly level course, through a patch of woodland and on to the alp of Wannelen (1624m). (This alp is served by a local cable-car from Ribi.)

Soon after leaving Wannelen the trail enters woodland and turns a spur of mountain to enter the Brunnital. The descent to Trogenalp begins with fine views glimpsed through the trees ahead. Trogenalp is a scattered collection of huts and summer-only dwellings perched on a sloping shelf of hillside with the great wall of mountains at the head of the valley forming a dramatic backdrop.

The trail continues, and about 45 minutes later comes to the hamlet of Nider Lammerbach (1516m). Just beyond cross a stream and head through woods as you make the descent to Brunnialp (1402m *refreshments*) with its pretty chapel set to one side of the chalets and cattle byres. Brunnital sits at the head of the valley and you can either walk down to Unterschächen by the road (about one hour), or take the footpath (signposted just below the hamlet). The path goes down the left-hand side of the stream, the road follows the right bank.

Chapel at Brunnialp

Route 43:	Unterschächen (995m) - Brunnialp (1402m) - Sittlisalp (1662m) - Unterschächen

Grade:	2-3
Distance:	14 kilometres
Height gain/loss:	667 metres
Time:	4½-5 hours
Map:	L.S. 246 Klausenpass 1:50,000

The little Brunnital is one of the loveliest valleys in Central Switzerland. Indeed, it would stand comparison with the best in all the Swiss Alps. It's not a major valley and remains largely unknown to the great majority of walkers in the Alps. But perhaps that is to its credit.

It runs south to north, draining a stupendous amphitheatre of mountains before flowing into the Schächental, and in some respects shows an affinity with the better-known valley of Lauterbrunnen in the Bernese Alps - with dramatic steep-sided walls down which waterfall ribbons hang in tassles of spray. There are mid-height

113

shelves of pasture on either side adorned with alp hamlets (some of which were visited on Route 42). There's forest and open meadowland in the valley itself, and a jaunty river scurrying through. And there's a magnificent headwall of mountains rising some 1600 metres above the last alp hamlet, a great upthrusting wall of stone with modest chokers of ice and permanent snow, and teasing hidden corries that taunt with their mystery.

This walk produces an insight into some of those mysteries. It gives wonderful views and, though there is a certain amount of back-tracking to be done, those views are being constantly rearranged and perspectives altered.

Begin in the main street of Unterschächen by Hotel Alpina and head south into the Brunnital. Follow the narrow road for about 1.5 kilometres until it swings left to cross to the true right bank of the river. (**Note**: it is possible to drive to this point, but no farther - permit-holders only may take their vehicles beyond. There's plenty of parking space just across the bridge.)

Do not cross the bridge but continue straight ahead on a broad path/track with the river to your left. (Brunnialp is 45 minutes from here.) The way is clear and views ahead enticing. Wander through forest until the track forks to allow the left branch to cross the river. Continue ahead and as you do so you can see a fine waterfall on the opposite side of the valley through the trees. In a patch of open pasture you pass an isolated alp farm, and soon after the track becomes a surfaced road that winds up to Brunnialp (1402m; *refreshments*).

Brunnialp is delightfully set at the head of the valley whose length it commands. It has a number of buildings - mostly hay barns, cattle byres or farmsteads - but there's also an attractive chapel and a small house serving refreshments.

Go into the hamlet and by the restaurant bear half-right on a waymarked trail signposted to Sittlisalp and Griesstal. A short distance up the slope branch off to the right at another signpost giving 45 minutes to Sittlisalp. This path climbs quite steeply up the hillside and in about 30 minutes from Brunnialp it forks. Head to the right, climbing a little higher, then the gradient eases and you come to

Sittlisalp (1662m) which has an incongruous sign directing you along the hillside to Sittlisalp in 30 minutes! This, however, refers to the hamlet shown on the map as Vord. Boden (1635m) where there is a simple cable-car link with the valley.

Wander along the hillside following a track with another fine, though minor, rocky cirque on the left, and come to the alp buildings of Lauwi (1633m) where there is a junction of tracks. It is here that the return journey begins by taking a descending track to the right. However, it is worth delaying this descent to continue along the hillside a short distance to the last collection of buildings where an unsophisticated cable-car (more a baggage/goods hoist than a passenger vehicle) descends to the valley. Views are consistently outstanding.

Note: the map shows another path descending to Unterschächen beyond Vord. Boden. During research for this guide the path proved to be impassable. Do not attempt to follow it unless signposts have been reinstated to suggest it is once more usable.

Return to Lauwi (20 minutes) and descend on the track signposted to Unterschächen (1¹/₂ hours). It descends steeply in places, winding down to Brunnialp once more, and there you bear left on the path which heads all the way to Unterschächen.

Route 44:	Unterschächen (995m) - Brunnialp (1402m) - Stich-Fülen (2329m) -Strangmatt (1251m) - Erstfeld (472m)
Grade:	3
Distance:	18 kilometres
Height gain:	1334 metres
Height loss:	1857 metres
Time:	9 hours
Map:	L.S. 246 Klausenpass 1:50,000

This long and demanding day's crossing of the mountains from the Schächental to the Reuss valley is not for the faint-hearted. There's

115

much height gain and loss (some superb scenery too), but it can be shortened by about 650 metres and $1^{1/2}$ hours at the end of the day by taking a cable-car down from Ober Schwändi to Erstfeld. There is also an opportunity to break the crossing into a 2-day walk by spending a night in the Berggasthaus Strangmatt ($6^{1/2}$-7 hours from Unterschächen). A brief outline of the route only is given.

Above and to the south-west of Brunnialp the hanging valley of Griesstal provides the key to the crossing. The Griesstal is cupped by a horseshoe of ridges breached in a couple of places by walkers' passes. The Stich-Fülen is one of them, a gap in the south ridge of Hoch Fülen (2506m).

Head through the Brunnital as described under Route 43 as far as Brunnialp (1 hour 45 minutes; *refreshments*). Opposite the restaurant take the waymarked trail heading half-right across meadows and follow signpost directions up into the Griesstal, reaching a junction of trails at the huts of Vorder Griesstal (1909m; $3^{1/2}$ hours). Continue heading roughly westward and rise to Hinter Griesstal (2092m) beyond which the climb to Stich-Fülen becomes more severe. The pass is gained in about 4 hours 45 minutes from Unterschächen; superb high mountain views are a just reward for the effort required to reach it.

The descent is steep on the western side of the ridge and leads through the alps of Balmeten and Öfeli before reaching Berggasthaus Strangmatt about two hours from Stich-Fülen. There now follows a thirty minute descending traverse through forest heading north-west to Ober Schwändi (1113m) where there is the option of taking a cable-car down into the Reuss valley at Erstfeld. The alternative footpath route will take about 1 hour 45 minutes.

Other Walks in the Schächental:

The map shows numerous walking possibilities in and around the Schächental, of which the above is merely a representative handful. Long routes across the north-walling mountains are favoured by experienced mountain walkers, and backpackers could conjure some fine multi-day tours. By reversing some of the routes described under the Muotatal section, and combining them with others that return to either the Schächental or Urnerboden, such tours become a distinct possibility.

From **SPIRINGEN** or **BRUGG** (upvalley from Burglen) both steeply climbing paths and cableways provide access to the popular **CHINZIG CHULM** for a crossing to the **MUOTATAL** (grade 3 in both cases) in the footsteps of Suvorov. See Routes 37 and 38 above (described in the opposite direction).

Not a high crossing, but an ascent of a modest summit providing good views, especially north to the Urnersee, is the route from **SCHÄTTDORF** to **BALMETEN** (2414m) on the south side of the valley. The Haldi cableway reduces the 1900 metres of ascent by 600 metres without detracting from its pleasures. The ascent (grade 3; 3½ hours from Haldi) is made by trail through several alps, including **HIRZENBODEN, SAUMLI** and the upper **OBERFELD** before gaining the east ridge of the mountain between Balmeten and Hoch Fülen. (Allow 4 hours for the descent to Schättdorf.)

The **HALDI** cableway also allows for a less demanding half-day walk; downhill nearly all the way. This is a walk that leads from the upper cableway station over a grassy ridge to the north-east and descent from there through forest into the **RIEDERTAL**, coming down to **BURGLEN**. This would be a grade 2 walk of about 3 hours.

The Riedertal is also easily reached by way of the Witerschwanden-Eggenbergli cableway for more forest-valley walks, or on hillside trails that visit well-situated alps with views to the north, east and west.

URNERBODEN

Viewed from the Klausenpass the Urnerboden valley is seen in all its open, glacier-scooped beauty. But the glaciers that long-ago bulldozed the valley into its present classic U-shaped trench, have receded to the upper corries of Clariden, innocent-looking from the valley bed. From the pass the valley is rich with green splendour, pastures speckled with cattle in the shadow of a long grey wall terraced at mid-height - a terrace that is not always evident from below. The grey wall too, at first appears to be virtually unbroken, but as you grow acquainted with it and study it from below, so you begin to notice that

Urnerboden with Clariden behind

it comprises a great number of turrets and spires, of slabs and chimneys reminiscent of the Brenta Dolomites - enough sport here to keep a rock climber happy for many a long day.

Below the pass, and to the south of the road, is the valley headwall of Klus (or Chlus) down which a waterfall cascades, draining the glacier and snowfields of Clariden (3268m) that towers above. The stream is the Fatschbach which flows north-east through the valley, crosses the cantonal boundary (Uri to the west, Glarus to the east) and then descends in a series of falls to the valley of the Linth, at whose head stands the Tödi.

While the northern slopes of Urnerboden are virtually devoid of trees, the southern flanks are adorned with a broad line of dark green pinewoods, the Wangiswald. Above them run the Gemsfairenstock and its subsidiary ridges which contain minor hidden valleys that drain not into the Urnerboden valley, but eastward into the Linth. Downstream in the valley of the Linth is the main village, Linthal, from whose adjacent village of Matt there runs a funicular up to the traffic-free resort of Braunwald.

Route 45:	Urnerboden (1372m) - Zingel (1756m) - Point 1788.9m

Grade:	3
Distance:	2 kilometres
Height gain:	416 metres
Time:	1½ hours
Map:	L.S. 246 Klausenpass 1:50,000

As a short, but rather strenuous, introduction to Urnerboden, this walk leads to a viewpoint from which the whole valley is laid out for inspection. It involves a very steep ascent of a vegetated gully to reach the alp of Zingel on the northern mountainside, followed by a high-level traverse of a hillside terrace in order to gain a dramatic perch from which to enjoy a splendid panorama. Unfortunately it will be necessary to retrace your steps for the descent to the valley.

Start the walk in Urnerboden, on the down-valley side of Hotel Wilhelm Tell. A series of *Bergweg* waymarks (white-red-white) head up a steep hillside alongside a fence, aiming for a slope between two great bastions of rock. (Superb wild flowers here before the scythe is put to work.) A path becomes more evident as you gain height, and in about 45 minutes you come onto a high shelf of hillside and bear right to reach the few huts that represent the alp of Zingel. Views from here are especially fine across the valley to Clariden; also to the walling rock faces immediately above the alp and stretching north-eastward.

The path becomes lost at this alp, but if you head across to, and beyond, the small buildings at the far left of the alp, the continuing trail will be found. It takes you initially well away from the edge of this hillside terrace, but then crosses the head of a deep gully or two, narrow and somewhat exposed, before bringing you onto a broad, high meadowland bluff rich in flowers, and with magnificent views.

Warning: do not stray too close to the edge as it plunges almost sheer for more than 400 metres.

As there is no continuation of the path return by the same route.

Zingel Alp above Urnerboden

Route 46:   **Urnerboden (1372m) - Zingel (1756m) - Läcki (1920m)**

Grade:	3
Distance:	2 kilometres
Height gain:	548 metres
Time:	1½ hours
Map:	L.S. 246 Klausenpass 1:50,000

This is a variation of Route 45, another short but steep walk to the high shelf of hillside on the northern side of the valley where fine views are to be had of the valley itself. Used in conjunction with that earlier route it would give an added boost to the walk, while in itself it makes a worthy half-day outing. Early in the summer the meadows are extravagant with alpine flowers.

Follow directions for Route 45 as far as Zingel, but as you come to the alp bear left and wander up the slope aiming for an obvious grassy saddle above to the left. There is no path at first, and no waymarks either, but as you gain height so you will come to a stony trail winding upwards. (Part of the route to the pass of Firner Loch.) This trail, however, disappears and you must make your way as best you can, emerging at last onto the saddle where you will find a low building and a signpost. This is Läcki (1920m).

From the rough pastures, pocked with limestone rocks and bright with alpine flowers, grand views are to be had, especially upvalley, while the craggy slopes above, in the direction of Firner Loch, are enticing to those of us who love wild mountain country.

Note: the signpost suggests a trail to the neighbouring alp of Firnen (20 minutes). The alp can be seen from the meadows, and the way is blazed with *Bergweg* paint marks heading south-westward. Most of the route is straightforward, but there is a succession of steep gullies to cross and in places the path is narrow and extremely exposed. On no account should you attempt to cross these gullies after rain (when the rocks are greasy) or if you feel at all unsure of your footing. Instead be content with the views from the meadows at Läcki and then return to Urnerboden by reversing the upward route.

Route 47:	Urnerboden (1372m) - Firner Loch (2248m) - Bisistal (1149m)

Grade:	3
Distance:	8 kilometres
Height gain:	876 metres
Height loss:	1099 metres
Time:	5 hours
Map:	L.S. 246 Klausenpass 1:50,000

A classic crossing from Urnerboden to the main tributary valley feeding the Muotatal in canton Schwyz, this is a fairly long, strenuous walk which should only be tackled in settled conditions and with good visibility.

Follow Route 46 as far as Läcki (1920m; 1¹/₂ hours). The signpost here directs you up to the west on a path that can be clearly seen slanting towards grey screes and rock walls that guard the pass. The pass is situated in a rocky crest to the west of the Läckistock (reached in about 30 minutes from the pass itself). Firner Loch is gained some three hours after leaving Urnerboden. Ignore the trail which goes north-eastward (to the Glattalp Hut) and instead follow the westerly trail. This leads in a steep descent via the huts of Gwalpeten (1522m) down alongside a stream, eventually onto a farm road that goes directly into the Bisistal at Sahl where there is a possibility of accommodation. (The nearest *gasthof* is at Schwarzenbach, about 3 kilometres downvalley along the narrow road.) Consult the Muotatal section for further details of accommodation, public transport etc.

Route 48:   **Urnerboden (1372m) - Braunwald (1256m)**

Grade:	2-3
Distance:	11 kilometres
Height gain:	145 metres
Height loss:	261 metres
Time:	3 hours
Map:	L.S. 246 Klausenpass 1:50,000

As has already been mentioned Braunwald is a traffic-free health resort perched upon a grassy terrace above the Linthal valley, and is reached by way of a funicular from Matt, near Linthal's railway station. The village faces east and south with views of the Hausstock massif across the valley. There is plenty of accommodation to be had in Braunwald, including a youth hostel.

This walk rises onto that hillside terrace in a long and easy traverse from the valley of Urnerboden, and makes much of the views.

Walk downvalley from Urnerboden village alongside the valley road for about three kilometres to the hamlet of Unterst Wang (1317m; 40 minutes). Take the path rising north-east to Vorder Stafel (1399m) in another half an hour. The continuing trail now deserts Urnerboden's valley by turning the corner below the projecting flanks of the Ortstock and rises to the highest point of the walk at

Usser Alp (1517m). Beyond this slope down to the alp huts of Rietberg (1362m; 2 hours 15 mins). A choice of route now becomes available. Either strike off to the left on a path to Braunwald, or continue ahead a little farther to join a farm road coming from Nussbüel. If taking the latter option (slightly longer than the footpath route) bear left on the road and follow it to Braunwald.

To return to Urnerboden by public transport, descend from Braunwald (footpath or funicular) to Linthal, and take the Postbus from there

Route 49:	Urnerboden (Klus; 1690m) - Gemsfairenhüttli (1951m)

Grade:	1
Distance:	3 kilometres
Height gain:	261 metres
Time:	1 hour
Map:	L.S. 246 Klausenpass 1:50,000

An easy walk along a service road to a farm whose meadows overlook the valley, this makes an ideal family stroll, while for those with more energetic inclinations an extension of the route will lead to a ridge with long views (Fisetengrat) or even to the Clariden Hut on the far side of the Gemsfairenstock.

Upvalley from Urnerboden the Klausenpass road makes a long loop south to a flat meadow below a rocky headwall down which a fine waterfall drains the upper snowfields and glaciers of Clariden. This sub-valley is known as Klus (or Chlus). There is a Postbus stop here, and also sufficient room to park a few cars. The walk begins at the bridge over the Fätschbach stream (signpost) where a farm road winds up the hillside to the east, then south. Wander along this road which soon makes a switchback and heads north, passes through a short tunnel and eases round the hillside. Views open and extend throughout the valley, the mountain wall on the far side looking particularly fine. In an hour from the Klausenpass road you reach the Gemsfairenhüttli with its meadowland beyond, a pleasant place to sit and enjoy the views.

For those who wish to continue to the Fisetengrat (a further hour from here), simply follow the trail which extends from the end of the farm road. It brings you to the northern ridge of the Gemsfairenstock from which point another trail descends to the valley. However, if you cross the ridge at the Fiseten Pass the continuing trail leads to the Clariden Hut in another three hours.

Route 50:	Urnerboden (1372m) - Klausenpass (1948m) - Unterschächen (995m)

Grade:	**2-3**
Distance:	**12 kilometres**
Height gain:	**576 metres**
Height loss:	**953 metres**
Time:	**4¹/₂ hours**
Map:	**L.S. 246 Klausenpass 1:50,000**

This is a splendid crossing from the valley of Urnerboden to the Schächental which forms a section of the Alpine Pass Route referred to elsewhere within these pages. It has its strenuous moments, but on the whole it is not too energetic and allows time to enjoy the many different aspects of the landscape through which the walk passes. Refreshments are available on the Klausenpass itself, reached about 1 hour 45 minutes from the start.

Leave Urnerboden heading upvalley alongside the road for about 1500 metres where, having rounded the first hairpin bend, a waymarked short-cut is seen directing you up a grass bank onto the next level section of road. As you gain height so more waymarks lead up among trees and over grass slopes; each footpath alternative to the road is worth taking. One long section over an open hillside provides especially fine views down into the valley falling far below. This trail brings you onto the road again at another hairpin section marked on the map as Vorfrutt (1779m). Here you walk down the road a few metres, cross a stream and then leave the road for a track signposted on the right. This climbs in easy zig-zags to high pastures well away from the road, and brings you to the Klausenpass *(refreshments)*.

To continue the walk down to Unterschächen follow the trail described under Route 41. This will take from $2^{1}/_{2}$ to 3 hours from the pass and on the way passes through the delightful alp hamlet of Äsch.

MADERANERTAL

Position:	South of the Schächental and east of the valley of the Reuss.
Maps:	L.S. 256 Disentis 1:50,000
	L.S. 246 Klausenpass 1:50,000
Bases:	Amsteg (511m), Bristen (770m), Golzern (1423m)
Tourist Information:	Information Uri, Gotthard-Raststatte, 6467 Schättdorf-Uri (Tel: 044 25 353)

Born among the glaciers of Clariden and the Chammliberg, the Maderanertal is a gem of a valley. It has no real resorts and Bristen, the only village worthy of the title in all its length, is small and compact and offers little in the way of accommodation or tourist attractions. But where the valley scores is in its untarnished landscape quality, the juxtaposition of limestone crags and steep sloping pastures, its streams and, particularly towards its head, the long and slender waterfalls that pour from high shelves to swell the Chärstelen torrent. It's a valley of pristine beauty; a valley rich in alpine flowers and crystals, among which there are some delightful walks to be had.

At the head of the valley the glacial snout of the Hüfifirn noses between the rocky portals of the Chli (or Kleine) Ruchen (2944m) and Grosse Düssi (3256m). Beyond those stony barriers the glacier is cradled by encircling ridges, while the valley itself rises on its northern flank to the jutting peaks and towers of the Windgällen massif. There are no short and easy ways over that massif to gain the Brunnital and Schächental beyond, but the natural terraces that relieve the steepness of its slopes offer some magnificent walking possibilities.

The southern slope of the valley is walled by the projecting ridges of the Oberalpstock and Witenalpstock, the first of which rises above small icefields to attain a height of 3328 metres, the second, at 3016 metres, guards the entrance to a tributary glen, the Etzli, at whose

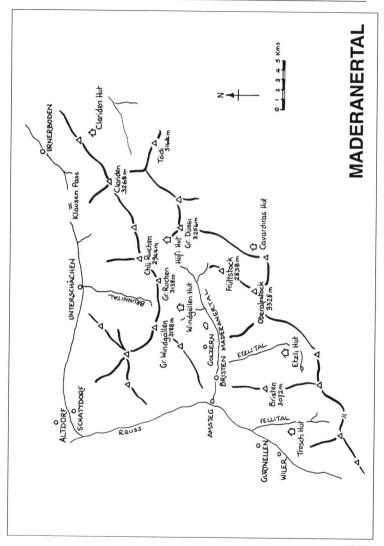

MADERANERTAL

URNERBODEN

Clariden Hut

Tödi 3146m

Klausen Pass

Clariden 3268m

Gr. Düssi 3256m

Cavardiras Hut

Chli Ruchen 2944m

Höfi Hut

UNTERSCHÄCHEN

BRUNNITAL

Gr. Ruchen 3138m

Windgällen Hut

Frültstock 2838m

Oberalpstock 3328m

Gr. Windgällen 3188m

GOLZERN

ETZLITAL

BRISTEN MADERANERTAL

Etzli Hut

ALTDORF

SCHATTDORF

Bristen 3072m

REUSS

AMSTEG

FELLITAL

Tresch Hut

GURTNELLEN

WILER

127

head two walker's passes offer routes over the mountains to the valley of the Vorderrhein.

At its western extremity the Chärstelenbach scores through a tight little gorge before flowing into the Reuss at the village of Amsteg. Amsteg itself is on the main Gotthard railway (its station is Amsteg-Silenen) and a Postbus service climbs steeply from there into the Maderanertal by way of a narrow road to the end of the tarmac about 2 kilometres beyond Bristen where there is cable-car access to Golzern, a charming hamlet 600 metres above the bed of the valley. Bristen also has a cable-car to Waldiberg, an alp overlooking the Reuss gorge.

These two cable-cars obviously attract a number of family visitors to the valley, but mostly the Maderanertal suggests a splendid isolation. One may walk its footpaths in solitude and enjoy the delightful views without distraction. It's a valley whose secrecy is jealously guarded by those who know it best, and one that remains largely unknown and unvisited by the majority of holiday-makers in Central Switzerland.

Main Valley Bases:

AMSTEG (511m) is not actually in the Maderanertal, but is situated at its mouth in a darkened curve of the Reuss valley on the old Gotthard road. It's only a small village with a modest amount of accommodation and limited shopping facilities. It does, however, have good road and rail access with the rest of Central Switzerland and, for walkers without their own transport, provides a convenient Postbus link with Bristen and the valley station of the Golzern cableway. This Postbus service runs from June to September (route 600.38).

BRISTEN (770m) straddles the road at the foot of the mountain whose name it shares, a short distance into the valley on the south bank of the river. It has a shop, PTT, restaurant, *Gasthofs* and *Matratzenlager* accommodation.

GOLZERN (1423m) has no road link with the valley but is reached in five minutes by cable-car. From its high position on the sunny, south-facing slopes, it enjoys some very fine views. Nearby

The slopes of the Rigi overlook the Lake of Lucerne (Routes 1-3)
Approach to the Surenen Pass (Route 14)

Trübsee below the Joch Pass (Routes 77-85-86)
Blackenalp (Routes 14-79-80)

Seewen (15 minutes' walk from the cable-car station) has a *Gasthof* and restaurant in a magical situation, with a small lake below that makes an idyllic site for a picnic.

Other Accommodation:
Beyond the metalled road, which ends at the valley station of the Golzern cableway, a dirt road continues for some distance linking a few small hamlets. Some accommodation is to be found here. At **LAGNI** there is a *Gasthaus* which offers rooms and *Matratzenlager*, and at **BALMENEGG** (1349m) an SAC hotel; both places occupy romantic woodland settings and are ideally placed for head-of-the-valley walks.

Mountain Huts:
There are four refuges of the SAC accessible from the Maderanertal: the **WINDGÄLLEN, HÜFI, CAVARDIRAS** and **ETZLI HUTS**.

The **WINDGÄLLEN HUT** (2032m) overlooks a gentle grassy basin at the base of the Windgällen crags, with lovely views to the south and east. Owned by the Academic Alpine Club of Zürich it has a guardian in the high season, when meals and drinks are available, and beds for about 46. A neighbouring hut can accommodate 38. It may be reached in about 2 hours from Golzern and is used by rock climbers as a base for routes on the Kleine and Grosse Windgällen, as well as by mountain walkers (tel: 044 650 88).

The **HÜFI HUT** (2334m) is reached in about $5^{1}/_{2}$ hours from Bristen (3 hours from Balmenegg). It is perched high on the rocks that form the gateway to the Hüfifirn, from where it looks into a wild glacial basin. The hut was built by the Pilatus Section of the SAC with bed spaces for 70 and has a guardian in residence from July until the middle of September, during which times meals and drinks are usually available. The telephone number for booking beds is 044 654 75.

Reached only by a very long and strenuous walk (about 6 hours from Bristen by way of the Brunnital below the Grosse Düssi - not to be confused with the Brunnital that flows into the Schächental) the **CAVARDIRAS HUT** (2649m) stands at the head of the Val Cavardiras in canton Graubunden. Owned by the Winterthur Section, it has 70 beds and a guardian at weekends in summer.

Largest of the four is the **ETZLI HUT** (2052m) with room for 110 in its dormitories. This is reached in about 4 hours from Bristen and stands near the head of the valley of the same name. A guardian is in occupation from the end of June to the end of September, with meals and drinks available then. The hut is owned by the Thurgau Section (tel: 043 3122 88). It is linked with the Tresch Hut in the delightful Fellital by way of the Pörtilücke (2506m).

Route 51:   **Golzern (1423m) - Golzerensee (1409m) - Golzern**

Grade:	**2**
Distance:	**3.5 kilometres**
Height gain/loss:	**14 metres**
Time:	**1½ hours**
Map:	**L.S. 256 Disentis 1:50,000**

Although this is only a very short walk - leading to a circuit of an idyllic mountain tarn - it is quite delightful and with enough features to entice you to dally. The lakeside makes a good site for a picnic, or perhaps to be lured into swimming in the water. In fact it's the sort of place in which to spend a lazy day simply enjoying the views.

From the upper cable-car station a signpost directs you north-eastward to the Golzerensee in 30 minutes. A broad and easy path heads along the hillside between sloping meadows with the pointed peak of the Grosse Düssi seen at the head of the valley. In about 15 minutes come to the hamlet of Seewen (*accommodation, refreshments*) and continue on the path which now slopes down towards the lake. Bear right when you come to a junction of paths just above it.

The Golzerensee lies in a scoop of hillside, partially skirted by forest, partially by meadows. With towering mountains to reflect in its waters, it offers a picturesque sight. Head round the southern shore, passing through a reedy area with a wooden catwalk, then up among trees. The path here is rough and involves some awkward manoeuvres for those unused to mountain trails (reason for Grade 2 rather than a straightforward 1). At the far end you overlook the tarn from a wooded bluff, then descend to meadows before following the path back to Golzern.

Route 52:	Golzern (1423m) - Windgällen Hut (2032m)

Grade:	3
Distance:	3 kilometres
Height gain:	609 metres
Time:	2 hours
Maps:	L.S. 256 Disentis and 246 Klausenpass 1:50,000

This is a "gold star" hut approach: a steep, somewhat strenuous walk - but what glorious views! Almost every step of the way is a delight of steep grassy hillsides full of flowers in early summer, big crowding mountains, deep valleys and distant tempting peaks. And the hut itself is set upon a superb high shelf of grassland with yet more delightful views, and with the steep grey face of the Windgällen rising behind it.

From the top station of the cableway take the path signposted to the Golzerensee, and after about 15 minutes you will reach the hamlet of Seewen *(accommodation, refreshments)*. The path goes through the hamlet, but immediately upon leaving it a signpost directs you to the left on a narrow path slanting up and across meadowland with the sharp peak of the Grosse Düssi seen ahead and with the small tarn of Golzerensee below to the right.

It's a fine walk which leads across meadows, through patches of forest, then cuts up steep slopes among alpenroses, minor streams and plenty of alpine flowers. The path is clear though narrow, and quite steep in places, but with a panorama of magnificent mountain scenery as you gain height.

Above the treeline the hillsides are glorious. About 1 hour 45 minutes from Golzern you will come to a large cairn standing just

Cairn below the Windgällen Hut

above the path which announces yet one more stunning viewpoint.
From it the hut is seen for the first time, and soon after passing the
cairn the path forks. Bear left and follow the trail climbing alongside
a stream which, in places, showers down in cascades. About 15
minutes from the path junction you reach the hut.

Allow 1¹/₂ hours for the descent by the same path, or combine it
with Route 53 below.

Route 53:	**Golzern (1423m) - Alp Stafel (1927m) - Tritt (1800m) - Maderanertal (Roadhead; 832m)**

Grade:	3
Distance:	13 kilometres
Height gain:	504 metres
Height loss:	1095 metres
Time:	5¹/₂ hours
Maps:	L.S. 256 Disentis and 246 Klausenpass 1:50,000

This is one of those high walks of which dreams are made; a walk to feed memories long after summer is over. It's among the best in this book for it offers one of the finest days out in all Switzerland. Choose a day of promise, take an early cable-car to Golzern and don't be hurried by the clock. There are so many places along the way that will make you want to throw off the rucksack and simply give yourself to the overwhelming beauty of the scene.

Take the path described for Route 52 as far as the junction of trails just beyond the large cairn referred to (1 hour 45 mins). Instead of heading left to climb to the Windgällen Hut, continue straight ahead along the path signposted to Alp Stafel, Tritt and Hotel SAC. About 10 minutes later you come to a second path junction where again you continue ahead. Alp Stafel is just above the path.

The trail now begins to descend, slanting gradually along the mountainside and enlivened by the glorious scenery. There are numerous streams to cross (caution required following a day of heavy rain); immediately after crossing one there is a fork in the path where you take the lower option (the upper path goes to Alp Gnof). Mostly the descent is gentle, but after the viewpoint of Tritt (1800m; 3 hours 15 mins) the trail goes down in long zig-zags towards the head of the Maderanertal where numerous waterfalls spray down the walls on both sides of the valley.

Come to another path junction (Sassalp 1465m) at the foot of the zig-zags and take the right-hand option, soon crossing a wooden bridge in the spray of a waterfall. Continue down among trees. In twenty minutes you will reach the collection of buildings that comprise Balmenegg (1349m), one of which is the SAC hotel.

Bear right, now on a broad track which soon brings you to the chalets of Balmenschächen (1185m). Here you cross the river to the left bank and wander down a dirt road that eventually reaches the valley station of the Golzern cableway. (On the way you will pass Gasthaus Lägni which offers refreshments, rooms and *Matratzenlager* accommodation.)

Route 54:	Bristen (770m) - Balmenschächen (1185m) - Hüfi Hut (2334m)

Grade:	3
Distance:	12 kilometres
Height gain:	1564 metres
Time:	5¹/₂ hours
Maps:	L.S. 256 Disentis and 246 Klausenpass 1:50,000

The way to the Hüfi Hut from Bristen allows a gradual unfolding of the valley's essential qualities. From gentle pasture to raw rock and ice scenery, the Maderanertal is stripped of its colourful veneer. This is a two-part walk. As far as the alp of Blindensee height is gained steadily, but thereafter a climb of almost a thousand metres makes for a demanding conclusion.

Leaving Bristen walk upvalley along the narrow metalled road and, where this finishes at the Golzern cable-car station, continue on the dirt road to Lägni and Balmenschächen (1185m; 1¹/₂ hours). Instead of crossing the river to the north (true right) bank, remain on the south side and follow the trail for a further 45 minutes to reach Blindensee (1375m), crossing the river on a bridge at Point 1259m.

The path continues upvalley beyond Blindensee and about 15 minutes later crosses the Chärstelenbach once more to begin the ascent of the western slopes of the Grosse Düssi. It's a strenuous climb of 2¹/₂-3 hours from here to the hut, but the path should be clear throughout.

Other Walks in the Maderanertal:
Maps of the region suggest numerous other walks and variations of walks throughout the valley. Among them the four-hour approach to the **ETZLI HUT** is worth considering. It begins a short distance upstream of Bristen where a bridge leads a track across the river and heads south into the Etzlital. From the end of the dirt road a trail continues along the valley before climbing to the hut which is found near the foot of the east ridge of the Steinstock. (Grade 3)

Another route which explores the length of the Etzlital is that which crosses the **CHRÜZLIPASS** (2347m) and descends south to

SEDRUN in the valley of the Vorderrhein. The route is the same as that for the Etzli Hut as far as Müllersmatt just below the hut. Then the trail cuts off to the east and climbs through the short Chrüzlital to gain the pass (5 hours). On the eastern side the way descends through the Valstrem and reaches Sedrun about $8^{1}/_{2}$ hours from Bristen. (Grade 3)

A fine two-day loop trip could be made by walking from Bristen to the **ETZLI HUT** where you spend the first night. Next day cross the Pörtilücke (2506m) to the west and descend to the **FELLITAL** (refreshments at the Tresch Hut), then continue downvalley to **GURTNELLEN** in the Reuss valley. (First day 4 hours; second day 6-$6^{1}/_{2}$ hours. Grade 3)

UPPER URI

Position: The headwaters of the Reuss, with the valleys of Urseren, Oberalp and Fellital, bounded by the Furka, St Gotthard and Oberalp Passes.

Maps: L.S. 256 Disentis 1:50,000
L.S. 255 Sustenpass 1:50,000
L.S. 265 Nufenenpass 1:50,000

Bases: Andermatt (1444m), Hospental (1452m), Realp (1538m)

Tourist
Information: Verkehrsbüro, 6490 Andermatt (Tel: 044 674 54)
Verkehrsbüro, 6493 Hospental (Tel: 044 678 30)

Travelling south through the dreary gorge of the Reuss both road and railway emerge from tunnels and galleries into an open level plain, suddenly bright and spacious after the gloomy constrictions of the previous long haul from Altdorf. Here the mountain walls appear much less forbidding than before, standing back as it were, as if to be admired with the perspective of distance. Streams flow from them to swell the Reuss, but that major river, born among the granite wastes of the Gotthard Pass, is only one of several newly-sprung waters to bear the name. From the east comes the Oberalpreuss, from the southeast the Unteralpreuss and from the south-west the Furkareuss, each one converging in or near Andermatt before plunging northwards to collect more streams and then discharge them into the Vierwaldstättersee.

Unlike others visited elsewhere in Central Switzerland, those valleys above Andermatt that splay out like fingers from a glove are scantily clad in vegetation, as befits their advanced altitude. But they are not without their charms and in winter provide some fine opportunities for cross-country skiing and ski-tours that take in high passes, glaciers and modest summits. In summer marked footpaths offer plenty of scope to match.

It's a region of passage, of course. The St Gotthard Pass (2109m)

UPPER URI

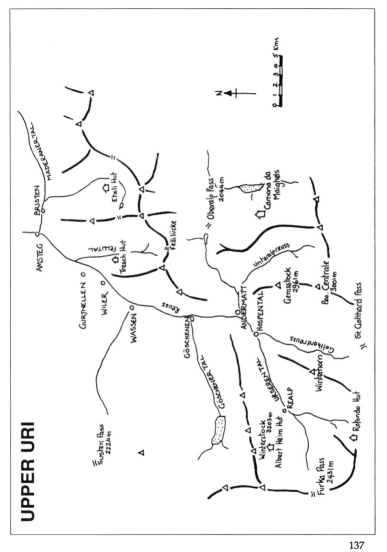

is one of the oldest and most famous of Alpine crossings whose ancient terrors have been subjugated by the world's longest road tunnel (16.3 kilometres), completed in 1980 after eleven years of construction. On its southern side beams the soft light of Ticino.

The Oberalp (2044m), which forms the boundary between cantons Uri and Graubunden (Grisons), though steep in ascent from Andermatt, is less formidable than the Gotthard and is adorned by a trout-filled lake near the summit. This pass too is crossed by both road and railway, the latter being on the route of the Glacier Express which links Zermatt with St Moritz.

Finally the Furka Pass (2431m) at the head of the Urserental is one of the highest road passes in Europe, from which a magnificent view is to be had of the Rhône Glacier. The railway tunnels through the mountains well to the south of the pass and emerges in the Goms valley of canton Valais. The road across the Furka, however, provides access not only with the Pennine Alps of Valais, but also with the Bernese Alps by way of the Grimsel Pass.

Main Valley Bases:

ANDERMATT (1444m) is by far the most important resort on the Reuss south of the Vierwaldstättersee. With a resident population of 1500 it is a bustling place with plenty of shops, restaurants, banks, PTT and a variety of hotels, *Gasthauser* and *Touristenlager* providing beds for a further 1500 visitors. (Contact the tourist office for their accommodation list.) Andermatt stands at an important railway junction, is also served by a number of Postbus routes and has a cable-car which rises in two stages to the 2961 metre Gemsstock.

HOSPENTAL (1452m) stands a little over 2 kilometres to the south-west of Andermatt and is noted for its thirteenth-century tower. The village was named after a former hospice at the foot of the Gotthard Pass road; fortunately the main road now bypasses it. Hospental has a youth hostel with 50 beds, a *Touristenlager* with 30 beds and 8 hotels offering a total of 150 beds. There are a few shops, a restaurant and PTT.

REALP (1538m) lies between Hospental and the Furka Pass and is a small village with a tragic history, for in the eighteenth century it was completely destroyed by avalanche. It has only limited shopping facilities, but for accommodation there is a choice of four hotels, two *touristenlagers* and a campsite a short distance downvalley towards Hospental.

Other Accommodation:
GÖSCHENEN (1106m) downvalley at the mouth of the lovely Göschener Tal, also has hotel accommodation, but is perhaps a little divorced from our designated Upper Uri region to warrant full inclusion in this section. But see the Göschener Tal section for full details.

There are hotels at the **FURKA PASS** and at **TIEFENBACH** on the approach to it, at the **ST GOTTHARD PASS**, and also on the **OBERALP PASS**.

Mountain Huts:
Several SAC huts are lodged in the mountains covered by this section.

The **ALBERT HEIM HUT** (2542m) is located high above Realp on the slopes of the Winterstock. Built by the Uto Section it can accommodate 100 in its dormitories and has a guardian during the main summer weeks from mid-July until the end of September. During this time meals and drinks should be available (tel: 044 677 45). The hut is reached on foot in about 2¹/₂-3 hours from Realp, or in 1¹/₂ hours from Tiefenbach on the Furka road.

On the southern mountains bordering Ticino the **ROTONDO HUT** (2571m) is accessible from Realp in 3¹/₂-4 hours by way of Hinterer Schweig and Oberstafel. It has 76 places and a guardian on the premises usually at weekends (tel: 044 676 16).

CAMONA da MAIGHELS (2310m) was provided by the Piz Terri Section (Ilanz). With bedspace for about 70 and a guardian usually from July until September, the hut is situated on the right-hand slopes of Val Maighels to the south of the Oberalppass, from which it is gained in about 2 hours.

North of the Oberalp, and reached by crossing the Fellilücke and descending into the Fellital, stands the **TRESCH HUT** (1475m) on the edge of woodland. A small hut with beds for 40, it was provided by the Albis Section. Meals are provided when the guardian is in residence, from mid-June to mid-October.

THE URSERENTAL

The waters of the Furkareuss and Witenwasserenreuss join forces south-west of Realp and channel north-eastward through the Ursenrental to Hospental and Andermatt. The bed of the valley is narrow, flat and pastoral, its northern wall rising steeply to a line of peaks that reaches its highest point on the Galenstock (3583m), which is part of the Winterberg massif whose eastern face overlooks the head of the Göschener Tal and whose western side spawns the great Rhône Glacier. The southern ridge of the Galenstock contains the Sidelenhorn, Grosse Furkahorn and Kleine Furkahorn before plunging to the Furka Pass. North of the Galenstock the ridge maintains its high elevation and comes to the Tiefenstock where a south-easterly spur cuts off to the Gletscherhorn, then runs roughly eastward to form the northern boundary of the Urserental.

South of the Furka a modest ridge closes the head of the Urserental, then swings more or less eastward above a clutch of small glaciers towards the St Gotthard Pass. Beyond the limits of this ridge lies Ticino.

It does not have the soft, seductive appeal of some of the lower valleys of Central Switzerland and is mostly used as a route of passage. There are no large patches of forest and but a few small tarns are to be found lodged in remote corries and on hillside shelves. Because of this the footpaths are likely to be far less busy than some others farther to the north, but those walkers who are not intimidated by seclusion will find plenty to attract them. The following outline routes are offered as a primer.

Route 55:	Realp (Tiefenbach; 2106m) - Albert Heim Hut (2542m)

Grade:	2
Distance:	2 kilometres
Height gain:	436 metres
Time:	1-1½ hours
Map:	L.S. 255 Sustenpass 1:50,000

This is a comparatively short, and not too demanding hut approach with the Winterstock providing a stark and rocky feature. Views from the hut are impressive both to the Winterstock and to the glaciers flowing from the Galenstock.

Either drive or take the Postbus (service 470.75) to Tiefenbach on the way to the Furka Pass. About 200 metres beyond the buildings a dirt road cuts off to the right. Walk along this and in another 100 metres bear left on a path and follow it for some way until it merges with another trail. This leads all the way to the hut.

Route 56:	Realp (Tiefenbach; 2106m) - Blauseeli (2136m) - Andermatt (1444m)

Grade:	3
Distance:	15 kilometres
Height gain:	160 metres
Height loss:	822 metres
Time:	5½ hours
Map:	L.S. 255 Sustenpass 1:50,000

The map shows a high belvedere trail running along the northern wall of the valley. This is known as the *Urschener Höhenweg*. It offers long interesting views and would make a fine day's outing. There are no opportunities for refreshment along the trail after leaving Tiefenbach, so go prepared with food and drink. Do not set out if there is a chance of bad weather as it is not always easy to break away from the route to make a fast descent to the valley in the event of a storm.

Take the Furka Pass Postbus (service 470.75) to Tiefenbach and join the track which breaks away from the pass road about 200 metres beyond the last buildings of the hamlet. Stay on the track as it climbs north-eastward to Gspenderboden (2266m), after which you descend some 200 metres on a path above Realp, then traverse the steep mountainside to reach the little tarn of Blauseeli in about 2½ hours. From here the trail continues to another small tarn, the Luterseeli (1976m), and then on to the alp hamlet of Rossmettlen (2091m 4 hours). The descent begins here, a long sloping trail that passes through Mülibach in the valley bed just to the west of Andermatt.

Route 57:	Realp (1538m) - Oberstafel (2220m) - Rotondo Hut (2571m)
Grade:	**2-3**
Distance:	**9 kilometres**
Height gain:	**1033 metres**
Time:	**3½ hours**
Maps:	**L.S. 255 Sustenpass and 265 Nufenenpass 1:50,000**

The Rotondo Hut of the Lagern Section of the Swiss Alpine Club nestles under the southern crags of the Tälligrat, a spur jutting north-eastward from the Stellibodenhorn. Above the hut is the small Witenwasseren Glacier; below it a glacial tarn. To the south rough slopes sweep up to the Witenwasserenstock and the ridge that undulates round to Piz Lucendro, beyond which lies the Val Bedretto in Ticino.

This approach to the hut is the most straightforward, as for much of the way it follows a minor road.

At the southern end of Realp, just beyond the church, a minor road breaks away from the Furka road and for a short distance runs parallel with the railway, then with the Furkareuss, rising steadily. At

Point 1603m the road crosses the stream at a hairpin and then climbs into the valley of the Witenwasserenreuss. In 45 minutes from Realp come to Hinter Schweig (1739m; *refreshments*). Continue on the road until it ends at Oberstafel (2220m; 2¹/₂ hours). (Along the way there is an option of taking a path to the hut which leaves the road at Point 2155m.) From the alp of Oberstafel follow the path which heads off to the right and climbs, steeply in places, for about one hour to reach the hut.

Note: From the Rotondo Hut experienced mountain walkers could cross the Passo di Cavanna (2613m) and descend to Villa in Val Bedretto, or by way of the Cavanna Pass traverse the southern slopes of Piz Lucendro, cross Passo di Lucendro (2532m) and descend to the St Gotthard Pass and from there make their way down to Andermatt for a three-day tour.

Other Walks in the Urserental:
One of the problems occasionally encountered by walkers in the valley is the temporary closure of some footpaths by the military authorities during exercises. The tourist office in Andermatt should be able to provide up-to-date information and advice.

Several walks are possible from the **FURKA PASS** region. One heads south from the pass to the moraines below the Mutt Glacier, then round via Bidmer and Gand and reaches **OBERWALD** at the head of the Goms valley. This Grade 3 walk will take about 4 hours. (Return by Postbus.)

Another, the **FURKA PANORAMAWEG**, leaves the road on the Urserental side of the pass and climbs over a shoulder of the Furkahorn 200 metres above the pass itself, then descends to the edge of the **RHÖNE GLACIER**. Fine wild mountain views of the Bernese and Pennine Alps, and of their glaciers, make this a popular walk (about 1¹/₂ hours).

The **GOTTHARD ROUTE** has been described elsewhere in this guide, but the section that goes from **ANDERMATT** to the **ST GOTTHARD PASS** - and continues to **AIROLO** in canton Ticino - is worth consideration by walkers based in the Urserental. See Route 18 for details.

There's a gentle valley walk which goes from **ANDERMATT** to **HOSPENTAL** and on to **ZUMDORF** (about 2¹/₂ hours; Grade 1), and several others that could be created by careful study of the map. Kümmerly & Frey publish a *Wanderkarte* for the area, entitled *Urner Oberland*. Basically this is an official Swiss Survey 1:50,000 map (L.S.) with walking routes overprinted in red and with outline directions (in German) printed on the reverse side of the sheet. It is available from some of the region's bookshops and tourist offices.

OBERALP

This short but steep little valley flows south-westward from the Oberalp Pass to the Urserental at Andermatt, a distance of a little over 6 kilometres (10.5kms by road). The upper region is typical pass scenery, a sombre lake, scant pasture rich in Alpine flowers, and far views. Below to the south-east the road descends by a series of hairpins to the valley of the Vorderrhein which scores a long trench through the mountains of Graubunden (Grisons). But south-westward the wall of mountains that lines the Urserental leads the eye to the Furka Pass; a jostling sea of peaks and a major route through them.

To the south twisted ridges hiccup between the valleys of Unteralp and Maighels, but to the north, directly above the pass, the saddle of the Fellilücke gives walking access to the lovely Fellital that projects northward into the Reuss.

There are no villages on the way to the Oberalp Pass, but there are a few collections of buildings and the slopes on either side of the road which writhes up from Andermatt are speckled with chalets and haybarns. Accommodation and refreshments are available at the pass.

There is no Postbus service across the Oberalp, but there are frequent trains from Andermatt (Furka-Oberalp line).

Route 58:	Oberalp Pass (2044m) - Fellilücke (2478m) - Tresch Hut (1475m) - Gurtnellen/Wiler (745m)

Grade:	3
Distance:	14 kilometres
Height gain:	434 metres
Height loss:	1733 metres
Time:	6-6½ hours
Map:	L.S. 256 Disentis 1:50,000

The Fellilücke is an easy saddle at the head of a delightfully peaceful and unfussed glen which links two major valley systems. The Fellital flows northward to join the Reuss downstream of Gurtnellen, a few kilometres short of the entrance to the Maderanertal, and is a real gem. This walk explores it from top to bottom and is one of the classic full-day outings of the region.

To gain the Fellilücke requires a comparatively short burst of effort from the Oberalp, and thereafter it's downhill all the way - physically, that is, for there's nothing second-best about the ever-varied descent through this fine valley. In losing more than 1700 metres of height during that descent there will be many changes to observe - scenically, geologically, botanically and climatically - all in a day's walk. And since this is a linear route one will need the assistance of public transport. Presuming your base is Andermatt, take the train to the Oberalp Pass for the start of the walk, and for a return at the end of the day catch the SBB train from Gurtnellen station (actually at Wiler) to Göschenen, and change there for the Furka/Oberalp line to Andermatt. Check time-tables before setting out, but you will invariably find that the change of trains at Göschenen is achieved within a few minutes; Swiss trains are, of course, supremely punctual.

From the Oberalp Pass station cross the road near Gasthaus Piz Calmut and walk down a narrow road between buildings as far as a stream. There you will find a signpost directing the path to the Fellilücke up steep grass slopes overlooking the Oberalpsee, steeply at times, then by way of rock steps to gain the first of a series of natural terraces. This terrace is of spongy grass with streams flowing through;

higher they are more stony and desolate and sometimes patched with snow. The trail of waymarks and cairns takes you first up the right-hand side, then crosses to the left with the obvious saddle of the pass ahead.

From the Fellilücke (2478m; 1¹/₂ hours) fine views are enjoyed of the wild-looking Fellital and its walling peaks. The descending path bears left round the head of the glen, and is then led by waymarks down through it, keeping a little left of centre, across rocks and snow patches, over boulder slopes and areas of avalanche debris. Eventually come to a charming oasis of grass and meandering streams (Murmetsbüel; 2010m), beyond which lie more rock-strewn obstacles. Here the path weaves first right then left and crosses the stream once or twice.

Continuing down-valley follow the stream as far as the pasture of Obermatt (1841m), behind which rises a rocky cirque given character by the spires and jagged ridges of the Sunnig and Schattig Wichel peaks. Passing to the left of the alp buildings cross the stream and continue down, now on the left bank. Within a few paces you come to the lip of the alp and gaze onto a lower section of the valley. The descent to it traces the course of the stream through a beautiful natural garden of alpenroses, juniper and bilberries straggling over rocks and boulders like balaclava helmets. Dwarf pine and numerous alpine flowers grow here. It's a lovely descent, and you soon come to more pastures and abandoned hutments (Hinter Waldi; 1531m).

Pass through another alp (Vorder Waldi; 1508m) and continue, now among trees, and a few moments later reach the Tresch Hut (1475m 4 hours; *accommodation, refreshments*), a sturdy stone-built mountain hut in a very pleasant location.

Note: An alternative route from Vorder Waldi crosses the stream and climbs through the hanging valley opposite to gain the Portilücke (2506m). The descent on the east side goes down to the Etzli Hut (3¹/₂ hours) and on to Bristen in the Maderanertal (6¹/₂ hours). Consult the Maderanertal section for further details of this area.

Continuing beyond the Tresch Hut the way remains on the left of the stream and loses height steadily among trees. Waymarks later take you across the stream and return again to the left bank a little

The Tresch Hut in the Fellital

later. At Hutten (1264m) there are some small huts and a cattle byre; there's also a bridge over the stream, but we ignore this and follow the left bank all the way now to Gurtnellen. When you come to a narrow road at Felliberg (1127m) wander down it, taking footpath short-cuts where indicated. (The stream has cut a deep ravine and at this point you're at the mouth of the glen, but still high above the Reuss which flows at right-angles ahead.)

When the road meets another at a hairpin, continue ahead, soon pass beneath the main Gotthard highway by a tunnel, and reach the old road. Cross half-left ahead (with care) and about 150 metres upvalley take a footpath down to the right to cross the Reuss. Walk upvalley and come to Wiler. Head to the right on a track and right again on a road which leads directly to the railway station. (*Refreshments* available nearby.)

The Fellilücke Pass

Route 59:	Oberalp Pass (2044m) - Fellilücke (2478m) - Lutersee (2358m) - Andermatt (1444m)

Grade:	3
Distance:	12 kilometres
Height gain:	434 metres
Height loss:	1034 metres
Time:	4½ hours
Maps:	L.S. 255 Sustenpass and 256 Disentis 1:50,000

Another fine walk with a short uphill climb to start, but followed by a long descent to Andermatt, it's one that is tackled by more walkers than the previously described route, yet is still peaceful and uncrowded.

From the Oberalp Pass station follow the route to the Fellilücke as described under Route 58, taking about 1½ hours. Instead of crossing the saddle bear left on the alternative trail signposted to Lutersee, Nätschen and Andermatt. It traverses the slopes of the

Schneehüenerstock above the Oberalpsee and reaches the tarn of Lutersee (2358m) about 45 minutes from the Fellilücke. Passing above the tarn the route continues heading south-west and maintains altitude for some way. Joining a farm road you will come to the alp of Lochstafel about 2 hours 45 minutes after setting out. Remain on the road almost as far as Nätschen station, but then break away on a well-marked path that descends steeply to Andermatt.

Route 60:	Oberalp Pass (2044m) - Lai da Tuma (2345m)
Grade:	2
Distance:	4 kilometres
Height gain:	301 metres
Time:	1½ hours
Map:	L.S. 256 Disentis 1:50,000

Nestling below Piz Tuma near the mouth of the Val Maighels south of the Oberalp Pass lies the tarn of Lai da Tuma, one of the sources of the Rhine. From this insignificant birthplace one of Western Europe's great rivers flows for more than 1300 kilometres before it reaches the sea at Rotterdam. This walk gives an opportunity to visit that tarn.

On leaving the station at the Oberalp Pass walk south along the road, passing from canton Uri into Graubunden. After about 1 kilometre the road makes a sharp left-hand bend. Leave it here and take to a footpath heading off to the right (south). It hugs the lower slopes of Piz Nurschalas into the broad opening of Val Maighels, then begins to climb round a spur, behind which you come to the lake. (Allow a little over an hour for the return to the Oberalp Pass.)

Other Walks from the Oberalp:
A full day's walk beginning at the **OBERALP PASS** and ending in **ANDERMATT** goes by way of the Val Maighels (passing the Maighels Hut), crosses the **PASS MAIGHELS** (2420m), descends through the Unteralp valley and reaches Andermatt after about 6½ hours. (Grade 3)

A shorter version of the same walk, saving about an hour overall, crosses the **LOLENPASS** (2399m) about 2 kilometres to the north of the Maighels Pass.

Another route which explores the Val Maighels crosses the **BORNENGO PASS** (2631m) at its head, and descends to the **CADLIMO HUT** in canton Ticino. (See the guide entitled *Ticino* published by Cicerone Press, which covers the Cadlimo area.) This walk would occupy about 5^1/$_2$ hours from the Oberalp Pass. (Grade 3)

GÖSCHENER TAL

Position:	**North of the Urseren valley and west of the Reuss gorge, in canton Uri.**
Map:	**L.S. 255 Sustenpass 1:50,000**
Base:	**Göschenen (1106m)**
Tourist Information:	**Verkehrsbüro, 6487 Göschenen (Tel: 044 651 96)**
	Verkehrsbüro, 6490 Andermatt (Tel: 044 674 54)

The Göschener Tal is unquestionably one of the most beautiful and dramatic valleys of the whole region. High mountains generously daubed with snow and ice form a spectacular barricade at its western end. Glaciers snake down from the peaks into uncompromisingly wild boulder tips and moraines now being turned into natural rock gardens. Small pools lie trapped among the boulders. Deep green mossy cushions adorn the banks of streams that wind among them, and alpenroses blaze scarlet in early summer. Chamois roam the screes and marmots burrow on the very edge of creation.

There are mountain huts perched in dress circle seclusion that exploit the grandeur of this alpine wonderland, and the trails that lead to these huts reward those who take them with hours of delight.

A narrow road climbs for 10 kilometres through the valley from Göschenen to the dammed lake near its head. Beyond the lake, the Göscheneralpsee, the Chelenalptal projects north-westward, while the short tributary glen of the Dammareuss has been scooped out of the mountains south-west of the lake by glaciers that have now withdrawn under the Dammastock (3630m).

South of the Dammastock the Winterberg massif claims two more summits (Rhönestock and Tiefenstock) before the high ridge, which nowhere drops below 3000 metres, sweeps round to the south-east, then east to the Winterstock. From the Winterstock the ridge continues sloping roughly eastwards as the southern wall of the Göschener Tal - the same wall that forms the northern barrier to the Urserental - while the northern side of the Göschener Tal is split by the secondary

GÖSCHENER TAL

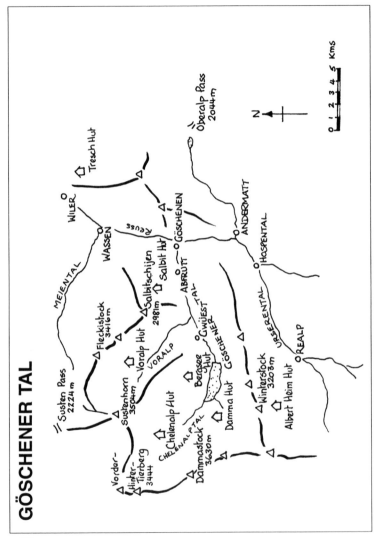

glen of Voralp.

The Voralp Tal is also blocked by glaciers. The Sustenhorn (3503m) is its highest summit. Icefields, broken by the steep nature of its eastern face, create a turmoil of seracs and crevasses above the valley, while the Steingletscher which flows from its western flanks flows into the head of the Gadmertal just below the Susten Pass.

The Voralpreuss discharges into the main Göschenertal below the rocky Salbitschijen (2981m). Here the valley is somewhat dark and wooded, but a little lower pleasant open pastures capture the sun with the river, the Göschenerreuss, flowing briskly down to Göschenen, below which it swells the Reuss itself.

Valley Base:
GÖSCHENEN (1106m) at the mouth of the valley is the only close practical village base for walking tours in the Göschener Tal - although walkers with their own transport could easily reach it by driving a short distance from Andermatt. Göschenen lies at the northern end of the 15 kilometres long St Gotthard railway tunnel, and has a large and important station. A Postbus (line 600.45) travels daily from the village to the Göscheneralp dam between late June and late October. It has a few shops, restaurants, PTT, a handful of hotels with around 100 beds and a youth hostel with 79 beds.

Other Accommodation:
At the **GÖSCHENERALP** roadhead (1715m) there's a large *Gasthaus* and restaurant. Downvalley a short distance from this the hamlet of **GWÜEST** (1585m) also has a *Touristenlager* with 40 beds.

Mountain Huts:
For practical purposes the valley gives access to five SAC huts, with a sixth (a bivouac hut) placed high on the west ridge of the Salbitschijen whose approach falls rather outside the scope of this guide.

The **SALBIT HUT** (2105m) is a base for climbers tackling various routes on the Salbitschijen. Provided by the Lindenberg Section, it has 60 beds and a guardian in occupation during weekends when meals are provided (tel: 044 654 31). A choice of paths lead to it from a short distance inside the valley, and demand no more than 2¹/₂-3 hours of approach.

The **VORALP HUT** (2126m) is approached by an easy path leading through the valley of the same name in about 2-2¹/₂ hours. It's a comfortable, well-appointed hut replacing a former refuge that was destroyed by avalanche in 1988. Owned by Section Uto, it has 40 beds. A guardian is usually on duty in summer to provide meals.

The **BERGSEE HUT** (2370m) was built in 1966 by the Angenstein Section from Basle, and has subsequently been enlarged. It stands high above the north bank of the Göscheneralpsee on the slopes of the Bergseeschijen. With spaces for 56 in its dormitories it is easily reached from the roadhead in 1¹/₂-2 hours. It's a popular hut and with a guardian in residence from June until October to provide meals (tel: 044 654 35).

Overlooking the Chelengletscher from an elevated position near the head of the valley, the **CHELENALP HUT** (also spelt Kehlenalp; 2350m) can accommodate 80 and has a guardian during summer weekends when meals and drinks are available. The hut is owned by Section Aarau and is reached in about 3¹/₂ hours from the Göscheneralpsee dam.

Finally, the **DAMMA HUT** (2438m) commands a view of the vast east wall of the Winterberg and is reached in 3 hours from the roadhead at the dam. Owned by the Lucerne-based Pilatus Section it can sleep 30 and has a guardian from mid-July until the end of August. Meals and drinks may be available during this time (tel: 044 657 81).

Route 61:	Göschenen (1106m) - Gwüest (1585m) - Göscheneralpsee (1797m)

Grade:	**2**
Distance:	**9 kilometres**
Height gain:	**691 metres**
Time:	**2¹/₂-3 hours**
Map:	**L.S. 255 Sustenpass 1:50,000**

Wandering through the valley enables one to absorb its many charms; the meadows and chalets, woodlands and streams and flowers - and all the time drawn by the imposing mountains that rise at its head.

In Göschenen walk away from the Reuss valley highway along the road which projects towards the Göschener Tal, keeping to the left of the stream. When the road swings to the right to cross the Göschenerreuss continue ahead on a path alongside forest, with the stream still on your right. The trail remains on the south bank (true right bank) practically all the way, although there are several bridges providing opportunities to cross to various hamlets that line the road.

After about 1 hour 15 minutes come to Bonen (1321m) opposite the entrance to the Voralp Tal, and one hour later you will reach Jantelboden in the valley below Gwüest. The way continues, then goes over the stream and climbs to the road, which it crosses. For the final stretch to the dam the path follows the road, but a little higher, and rejoins it just before the Gasthaus/restaurant below the dam.

Route 62:	Göscheneralpsee (1797m) - Vorder Röti (1813m) - Point 1986m -Göscheneralpsee

Grade:	2
Distance:	7 kilometres
Height gain/loss:	189 metres
Time:	3 hours
Map:	L.S. 255 Sustenpass 1:50,000

A justifiably popular walk, this makes a circuit of the Göscheneralpsee and offers superb views of numerous high snow- and ice-clad peaks.

Begin at the Postbus terminus by the Gasthaus below the dam. At a signpost indicating the route to the Bergsee, Damma and Chelenalp Huts head to the right on a clear path rising easily among shrub-covered granite slabs. Making height without much effort, in about 20 minutes you will come to the first of many fine viewpoints and gaze directly at the peaks of the Winterberg, with their glaciers sparkling from a cirque that heads the short glen of the Dammareuss.

After about a kilometre the path forks. Continue straight ahead (signposted to the Damma and Chelenalp Huts), soon gaining a view onto the lake below.

From this point the path begins a steady descent towards the western end of the lake where you gaze directly up the Chelenalptal to the Tierberg peaks. In the mouth of this glen the alp hut of Vorder Röti (1813m; 1¹/₂ hours) is seen on the far side of the Chelenalpreuss. At a path junction near the bridge over this stream bear left, cross the bridge and follow the trail as it leads among alpenroses and alder scrub, then begins to climb a rocky slope. Rising steadily you come to the mouth of the Dammareuss glen, then cross to the left-hand side of some large boulder slabs (caution when wet) from where there is a very fine view up to the Dammagletscher and its headwall of peaks curving in a great amphitheatre high above.

Walk up the wild and stony valley with the glacial torrent thundering to your left, and cross the torrent at a bridge. The path on the east side of the stream slants at a comfortable gradient up the hillside, crossing a number of minor streams on the way.

As the path approaches the mountain spur around which you leave the Dammareuss glen (Point 1986m), the way steepens a little. At the high point pause to enjoy the superb views behind you. Now the trail starts to descend among alpenroses and over yet more streams. Pass the mouth of a short glen which rises to the Lochberg, cross its boisterous stream and continue round the lake to the dam. Go over the dam and descend to the *Berggasthaus* at the roadhead.

Route 63:	Göscheneralpsee (1797m) - Bergsee Hut (2370m)
Grade:	3
Distance:	2.5 kilometres
Height gain:	573 metres
Time:	1¹/₂-2 hours
Map:	L.S. 255 Sustenpass 1:50,000

From the roadhead below the dam follow directions as for Route 62

The Winterberg Massif seen above the Göscheneralpsee

for about one kilometre as far as the path division where there is a signpost indicating the way up to the Bergsee Hut. Bear right and climb, gently at first, but more steeply as you gain height, and so reach the hut without difficulty.

Route 64:	**Bergsee Hut (2370m) - Chelenalp Hut (2350m)**
Grade:	3
Distance:	4 kilometres
Height loss:	20 metres
Time:	3-3½ hours
Map:	L.S. 255 Sustenpass 1:50,000

Both these huts occupy elevated positions high above their valleys, and enjoy superb views. This route linking the two extends those views as it maintains altitude along the mountainside. The route is not marked on some L.S. maps, but is outlined on the *Urner Oberland*

Wanderkarte (published by Kümmerly & Frey) available locally.

From the Bergsee Hut the way skirts the southern shore of the Bergsee tarn, then climbs to the Vorder Mur, a shoulder of the Bergseeschijen. From here it makes a lengthy traverse of the Hinter Mur which lines the Chelenalptal, reaching a point above the Chelenalp Hut, but below the glacial napkin draped down the face of the Sustenlimihorn. A steep descent then takes you down to the Chelenalp Hut.

Route 65:	Göscheneralpsee (1797m) - Chelenalp Hut (2350m)

Grade:	3
Distance:	6.5 kilometres
Height gain:	563 metres
Time:	3^{1}/$_{2}$ hours
Map:	L.S. 255 Sustenpass 1:50,000

A fine approach and a boldly situated hut, this walk will provide a very pleasant day in the mountains. Choose a bright morning, take your time as you wander through the valley and enjoy its many different aspects, relax with a drink and a meal at the hut, then slowly walk back down again. You'll be well-rewarded.

Follow directions as for Route 62 as far as the path division in the mouth of the Chelenalptal near the hut of Vorder Röti (1813m; 1^{1}/$_{2}$ hours). Instead of crossing the bridge continue ahead, following the path into the valley to the right of the stream. It leads over rough meadowlands bright with alpenroses in early summer, with streams snaking through and wild flowers lining boggy patches. There are also stony regions inhabited by marmots, and rising and falling the trail provides a chance to spy on these furry creatures. As you continue upvalley so you pass the small hut of Hinter Röti (1941m) nestling below a boulder pile.

Towards the head of the valley the way becomes yet more stony, littered with rust-red rocks and the glacial tongue nearby stained by the same coloured grit from the mountains. Rising steadily the path brings you to a large granite slab shoulder with a substantial cairn perched upon it. This is Point 2127.8m and the hut is now directly above you, but more than 200 metres higher. The trail swings to the right and climbs steeply to reach it. Views are magnificent throughout.

Allow 2¹/₂-3 hours for the descent by the same path.

Route 66:	Göscheneralpsee (1797m) - Damma Hut (2438m)

Grade:	3
Distance:	6 kilometres
Height gain:	641 metres
Time:	3 hours
Map:	L.S. 255 Sustenpass 1:50,000

The Damma Hut is set in a spectacular position on a grass-cushioned mound of granite high above its stony glen, and with a direct view onto a cirque of glacier-clad peaks. The first hut was built here in 1915, but this has since been considerably enlarged and improved to accommodate climbers drawn by the many challenging routes that are to be tackled nearby. This approach to the hut is full of drama and beauty.

It begins by sharing the same path from the roadhead as Route 62, round the western end of the lake and into the glen of the Dammareuss. Then, where the path divides, instead of crossing the bridge to the east side of the glacial torrent (as per Route 62; 1 hour 45 mins), continue upvalley, but veering to the right. The path is well-made and well-marked, rising over rock slabs with steps in places. Where it crosses rocky terrain making it difficult to create a proper path, there are plenty of waymarks to guide you. And all the time views ahead are stunning. The trail advances on a long, steadily-rising westward traverse of the slopes of the Moosstock, then twists north and climbs steeply to the hut.

Downvalley (south-east) the spiky crags of the Feldschijen and

Müeterlishhorn look fine; so too do the peaks that spawn the glaciers immediately to the south and west, rising to the Dammastock.

Allow a little over 2 hours to return by the same route, or 1¹/₂ hours by taking the path on the south side of the lake (see Route 62).

Note: An alternative approach to the Damma Hut would be to follow the lake circuit clockwise from the dam (ie. along the southern shore). This would be slightly shorter than the route described above.

Route 67:	Damma Hut (2438m) - Chelenalp Hut (2350m)

Grade:	3
Distance:	6.5 kilometres
Height loss:	625 metres
Height gain:	7 metres
Time:	3 hours
Map:	L.S. 255 Sustenpass 1:50,000

Walkers who may have stayed overnight at the Damma Hut are encouraged to visit the Chelenalp Hut whilst in the area.

Descend the steep path from the hut into the Dammareuss glen and wander down-valley towards the lake. The path veers left round some boulder slabs and descends steadily towards the western end of the Göscheneralpsee. Passing below the alp hut of Vorder Röti (1813m; 1 hour) cross a bridge over the Chelenalp stream and bear left into the Chelenalptal. The path from here (described under Route 65) takes you through the valley and in two hours brings you to the hut.

Route 68:	Göschenertal (Voralp; 1404m) - Voralp Hut (2126m)

Grade:	2
Distance:	6 kilometres
Height gain:	722 metres
Time:	2¹/₂ hours
Map:	L.S. 255 Sustenpass 1:50,000

The Damma Hut

The Damma Reuss flows from the Winterberg Massif

The Voralp Tal is dominated by the Sustenhorn (3503m), and the hut gazes across at its graceful form and the turmoil of glaciers that pour from it. The hut is a comfortable one, built in 1989 to replace the former building that was destroyed by avalanche the year before. On the approach to it you pass beneath the western crags of the Salbitschijen, a peak of comparatively modest altitude (2981m) that nevertheless holds certain appeal to rock climbers.

A little over 5 kilometres upvalley of Göschenen the road to the Göscheneralpsee makes a series of hairpins. At the first hairpin (Voralp) there is a Postbus stop and a lay-by parking space for several cars. The walk begins here and is signposted.

At once the path crosses the Voralpreuss and enters conifer woods that guard the entrance to the valley, but you soon come above them and rise steadily through the narrow V-shaped glen to the right of the stream. Clear and distinct all the way, the trail takes you through patches of rough rock-littered pastures, and in a little over an hour the valley curves to the right and you cross a more level pasture with the low alp buildings of Horefelli (1786m) ahead.

Beyond Horefelli the path climbs again to pass a bridge on the left, and continues directly ahead, still on the right of the stream. So gain a higher valley region where there are alpenroses and alder. Cross more rocky slopes and rise north-westward towards the head of the valley. Shortly after passing a rough hut on the opposite side of the stream (Flachensteinen; 1987m) the way steepens, and with some zig-zags brings you to the Voralp Hut.

Route 69:	Göschenen (1106m) - Abfrutt (1167m) - Salbit Hut (2105m)
Grade:	3
Distance:	5 kilometres
Height gain:	999 metres
Time:	3 hours
Map:	L.S. 255 Sustenpass 1:50,000

With more than 900 metres of height to gain in a little over 2 kilometres from the road, it will be obvious that this is a steep walk. Those who are heavily laden - climbers, for example, with rucksacks full of ironmongery and ropes - can sometimes arrange for their rucksacks to be carried by a small baggage cable-car from Ulmi to Regliberg. However, it is not for general passenger use.

The hut is perched on the steep slopes of the Salbitschijen with fine rock scenery above it. There is a hut-keeper in attendance usually during summer weekends.

From Göschenen walk into the Göschener Tal along the minor road that serves it. In about 30 minutes come to the hamlet of Abfrutt. (It is possible to take the Postbus to Abfrutt, or by request as far as Ulmi.) Continue along the road and, just beyond Ulmi at Point 1195m, take the path on the right which climbs steeply among trees for about 45 minutes to reach Regliberg (1680m; $1^1/2$ hours) and a junction of paths. The onward trail is signposted and well-marked. It continues to climb through woods, emerges from them at about 1800 metres and works a way up grass slopes to gain the hut.

Note: There are alternative routes of approach to this hut. One climbs steeply from Abfrutt and joins the path described at Regliberg. Another begins at Biel, a short distance from Göschenen, and climbs by way of Tschingel before making a long rising traverse to join the route described above at Trogengand. Both will take about three hours.

MEIENTAL

Position:	North of the Göschener Tal and west of the Reuss valley. The head of the Meiental is crossed by the Sustenpass.
Map:	L.S. 255 Sustenpass 1:50,000
Base:	Wassen (916m)
Tourist Information:	Verkehrsbüro, 6484 Wassen am Gotthard (Tel: 044 652 33)
	Verkehrsbüro, 6490 Andermatt (Tel: 044 674 54)

Traversed by the Sustenpass road the Meiental is an unsophisticated delight of which motorists catch merely a glimpse. Looking through it from the lower reaches one perceives a gentle valley of green pastures, weathered barns and chalets, with the majestic and aptly-named Fünffingerstock rising as an ice-draped barrier at its head. The old road through the valley makes for pleasant walking, while the "new" road is often a nose-to-tail stream throughout high summer.

Away from the pass road you stroll among cattle with clear mountain streams trundling past. In spring and early summer the meadows are bright with flowers; later they're mown and the heavy scent of drying hay hangs like an invisible cloud from one side to the other.

For the walker the Meiental is a valley of simple pleasures, and is worth taking a day or two to explore. Mindful that the walling peaks are beyond the scope of this guide there are, however, mountain huts to visit that provide a taste of high adventure. Those peaks that rise to the south-west hide the glen of the Voralptal described under the Göschener Tal section. Fine mountains they are, reaching between 3000 and 3400 metres and with small glaciers and snowfields draining out of high corries to add to the bounty of the Meienreuss. At their lower end the Rorspitzli throws out a long easterly spur with several summits poking from it before sloping steeply down to form one of the valley's gateposts above Wassen. At its upper end, marked by the

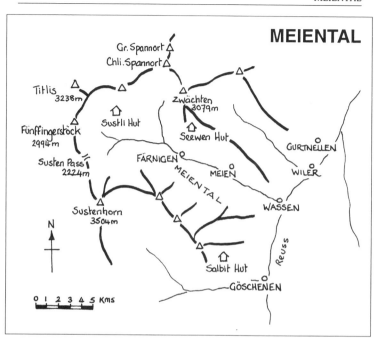

Stucklistock (3308m), a continuing ridge breaks away to the west to
the Kleine (or Chli) Sustenhorn where another projects northward to
close the Meiental with a wall of stone. This wall of stone, this closure,
has been breached by the tunnel of the Sustenpass.

Above the pass to the north rises the Fünffingerstock, part of a
beautiful craggy ridge of peaks whose northern slopes are heavily
glaciated and whose southern flanks are most attractively adorned
with snow and ice also. One of these headwall peaks, the Grassen
(2946m), incidentally, is linked by way of the Wendenjoch to the
Titlis.

As the headwall curves as a great amphitheatre, it rises to the
Kleine (or Chli) Spannort, the northernmost summit above the
Meiental. From here the ridge meets the Zwächten before heading

165

south and south-east in a long and steady descent to the valley of the Reuss.

It's all highly attractive and one may imagine that before traffic began to use the Susten, the Meiental must have been a real back-country gem. The first road over the pass was created in 1811 by the cantons of Bern and Uri to enable trade to continue between the Bernese and Italians without the necessity of crossing into the Valais, which had then been annexed by Napoleon as part of the French Empire. A hundred years earlier, during the Religious War, the Meienschanz redoubt was built above Wassen to protect Uri from the Bernese; it was destroyed by the French in 1799.

Valley Base:

WASSEN (916m) huddles at the mouth of the valley on the west bank of the Reuss. The village is noted for its lovely eighteenth-century hilltop church with domed spire and inlaid wooden altars. The Gotthard railway spirals through the mountainside nearby, while the motorway forms another, not altogether welcome, neighbour between the village and the river. Wassen has limited tourist facilities, but can accommodate about 50 guests in its 2 hotels.

Other Accommodation:

Elsewhere in the Meiental rooms are available at **MEIEN** (shown as Dörfli on the map) which has a *Gasthaus* and restaurant. The hamlet of **FÄRNIGEN** also has a single hotel.

Mountain Huts:

Just two SAC huts are within reach of walkers in the Meiental, the **SUSTLI** and **SEWEN HUTS**.

The **SUSTLI HUT** (2257m) stands on the steep hillside above the Gufer Alp in the upper part of the valley and is reached in about an hour from the road (5 hours from Wassen). Owned by Section Rossberg based in Zug, the hut can accommodate 100 in its dormitories. The guardian is in residence during the summer (June-September) to provide meals and drinks (tel: 044 657 57).

The **SEWEN HUT** (2148m) also stands on the northern hillside, but this time on the slopes of the Sewenstock. A little smaller than the above-mentioned hut, it can sleep 60 and has a guardian at weekends (tel: 044 658 72). Owned by the Pfannenstiel Section (Mannedorf) of the SAC, it is reached in 1¹/₂-2 hours from the entrance to the Chlialp glen on the Sustenpass road.

Route 70:	Wassen (916m) - Färnigen (1455m) - Guferplatten (1727m)

Grade:	1-2
Distance:	12 kilometres
Height gain:	811 metres
Time:	4 hours
Map:	L.S. 255 Sustenpass 1:50,000

This is one of those valley walks designed to introduce the visitor to the area in the gentlest possible manner. Height gain is made steadily. There are two places (Meien/Dörfli and Färnigen) where refreshment may be had along the way, and another restaurant on the road where a return to Wassen is possible by Postbus. Throughout views are quite charming.

The walk begins by wandering up the Sustenpass road for about 200 metres from the turn-off in Wassen. A signpost then directs you off to the left on the old road, where you wind uphill to the edge of forest and reach the remains of the historic Meienschanz. Continuing, come to a bridge (the Fedenbrugg) and cross the Meienreuss to the opposite bank and head up valley to Husen (1177m). The way continues and about 1¹/₂ hours from Wassen brings you to the hamlet of Meien/Dörfli (1274m; *accommodation, refreshments*).

Walk along the road until, just beyond the village name-board, a farm road (original valley road) slants off to the left heading almost parallel with the main road. It cuts between meadows and passes a number of farms that enjoy fine views to the Fünffingerstock. Rising a little you come onto a narrow surfaced road that takes you a few metres to the Hotel Edelweiss at Färnigen (1455m 2¹/₂ hours;

accommodation, refreshments).

Beyond Färnigen the way reverts to a farm track and then forks. The left-hand trail crosses the river, the continuing track stays on the north bank, but the two ways converge again further upvalley.

Guferplatten is situated on the curve of the valley where streams converge and views look up to the glacier of Chalchtalfirn coming from the ridge between the Kleine Sustenhorn and the Sustenspitz, while the road twists its way to the pass high above to the west. A path climbs from here up to the road at Chli Sustli (1907m) where there is a kiosk/restaurant and a Postbus halt for the return journey to Wassen.

Note: It is possible to extend the walk from Guferplatten over the Sustenpass (5-5$^{1}/_{2}$ hours from Wassen) and down to Hotel Steingletscher (6 hours) on the far side. A path leads from Steingletscher in 3$^{1}/_{2}$ hours to the Tierbergli Hut marooned among glaciers to the west of the Sustenhorn. But to complete a major crossing from the valley of the Reuss to the Haslital, a path continues down from Hotel Steingletscher through the Gadmental to reach Innertkirchen in 4$^{1}/_{2}$ hours. (For further ideas for walks in the Haslital and neighbouring regions, consult the guidebook *The Bernese Alps,* published by Cicerone Press.)

Route 71:	Meiental (Chli Sustli; 1907m) - Sustli Hut (2257m)

Grade:	3
Distance:	1.5 kilometres
Height gain:	350 metres
Time:	1 hour
Map:	L.S. 255 Sustenpass 1:50,000

A short but very steep climb takes you from the road to the Sustli Hut. Chli Sustli is reached by Postbus from Wassen. The stop to ask for is Sustenbrüggli.

The path begins at the sharp bend on the road, and climbs without diversion directly to the hut. An alternative approach is given as Route 72.

Route 72:	Wassen (916m) - Färnigen (1455m) - Sustli Hut (2257m)

Grade:	2-3
Distance:	12 kilometres
Height gain:	1341 metres
Time:	5 hours
Map:	L.S. 255 Sustenpass 1:50,000

A longer, but more satisfying, route than that outlined above, it gives the riches of contrast and provides a good day's walk.

Follow directions as given above for Route 70 as far as Färnigen (2¹/₂ hours). Continue ahead along the track, keeping on the north bank of the Meienreuss until it forks just after crossing a stream flowing from the Chlialp glen. Take the right fork and go up onto the Sustenpass road, and walk up the road for a little over a kilometre. A path then breaks away above the road and makes a long and steadily ascending traverse of hillside, eventually arriving at the hut.

Route 73:	Wassen (916m) - Färnigen (1455m) - Sewen Hut (2148m)

Grade:	3
Distance:	11 kilometres
Height gain:	1232 metres
Time:	4¹/₂ -5 hours
Map:	L.S. 255 Sustenpass 1:50,000

The Sewen Hut is used as a base by climbers tackling routes on the Sewenstock, Hoch Sewen, Miesplanggenstock and Schafschijen, or for such adventurous crossings as the Rot Bergli into the Gornerental.

A pleasant, sturdy hut with bedspace for about 60 and a guardian at weekends in summer.

From Wassen to Färnigen the walk is the same as that already described for Route 70 (2½ hours). Continue along the track, but immediately before it comes to the stream flowing from the Chlialp glen, leave it and climb a short path onto the Sustenpass road. On the opposite side of the road a signpost directs the continuing trail up to the hut. The way climbs at first among trees, then over open hillside, steeply up a spur to reach the hut in about 2 hours from the road.

MELCHTAL AND SARNER AA

Position:	In canton Obwalden. South-west of the Vierwaldstättersee and west of the Engelbergertal. The Melchtal flows northward into the valley of the Sarner Aa which slopes down from the Brünig Pass.
Maps:	L.S. 245 Stans 1:50,000
	L.S. 255 Sustenpass 1:50,000
	L.S. 244 Escholzmatt 1:50,000
	L.S. 254 Interlaken 1:50,000
Bases:	Lungern (752m), Sarnen (473m), Kerns (564m), Melchtal (890m), Melchsee-Frutt (1902m)
Tourist Information:	Verkehrsbüro, 6078 Lungern (Tel: 041 6914 55)
	Verkehrsbüro, 6060 Sarnen (Tel: 041 6640 55)
	Verkehrsbüro, 6064 Kerns (Tel: 041 6670 70)
	Verkehrsbüro, 6061 Melchsee-Frutt (Tel: 041 6712 10)
	Verkehrsbüro Obwalden, 6055 Alpnachdorf (Tel: 041 9626 26)

At a modest 1008 metres the Brünig Pass forms a boundary between cantons Bern and Obwalden - between the mountains of the Bernese Alps and those of Central Switzerland. Green mountains and an even greener valley project north-eastward, their streams uniting to become the Sarner Aa which flows into the Alpnacher See and thence into the Vierwaldstättersee. This valley, the valley of the Sarner Aa, gleams with water. Two medium-sized lakes (not counting the Alpnacher See) shimmer between low pastures, their shores clustered here and there with villages whose balconies are decked with flowers and the meadows fluffed with fruit trees.

The valley descends step-like from one levelling of pasture to the next, and with the bulk of Pilatus rising ahead. On the western side gentle mountain spurs nose down among forests into the pastures,

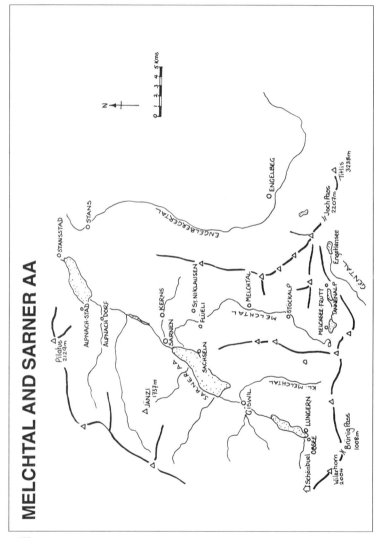

MELCHTAL AND SARNER AA

while the south-eastern flank is sliced by two tributary glens, those of the Klein Melchtal and the Gross Melchtal.

At the head of the Melchtal (more correctly the Gross Melchtal) a broad, high plateau, or basin, of scant meadowland adorned by two lakes provides an interesting base for a short walking holiday. Low ridges bound it on either side from which a handful of modest drag lifts and the Bonistock cable-car offer downhill sport to winter enthusiasts, while the gently sloping floor of the basin is ideal for cross-country, or *langlauf*, skiing. In summer those same low ridges are easily crossed on foot, and a variety of trails make the most of them, often reaching panoramic viewpoints that show not only the towering block of the nearby Titlis, but also the Wetterhorn and other easily-recognised peaks of the Bernese Oberland. Patches of limestone pavement, starred with a rich alpine flora, afford additional interest.

On this plateau lie the hamlets of Tannenalp and Melchsee-Frutt, only small clusters of buildings perhaps, but they are nevertheless capable of accommodating 1500 guests.

North of Melchsee-Frutt the Melchtal is drained by the Cheselenbach which pours through narrow defiles and over gentle alps on its journey to the Sarner See. By contrast with its upper levels, the valley is narrow and steep almost throughout its length, and is confined by mountains that never quite reach 3000 metres; mountains that often remain largely obscured from view by forests that clothe their lower slopes. On the far slopes of the western mountain wall the geographical centre of Switzerland is located on the Älggialp (1650m) above the Klein Melchtal.

The valley of the Sarner Aa is well-served both by railway (Lucerne-Brünig-Interlaken) and by Postbus. As for the Melchtal, a road into the valley begins at Sarnen, from where a Postbus (Line 470.25) provides a service as far as Stockalp, a distance of about 15 kilometres. From there a gondola cableway rises to Melchsee-Frutt, while the narrow continuation of the road is controlled by a timed one-way system: uphill for 40 minutes on each even hour, down for 40 minutes every odd hour. Day visitors to Melchsee-Frutt are obliged to leave their vehicles in a car park (fee charged) a short distance below the resort.

Main Valley Bases:

LUNGERN (752m) stands at the south-eastern corner of the Lungerer See with the nearby village of Obsee providing cable-car access to the panoramic viewpoint of Schönbüel (2011m). Lungern has two campsites and a choice of hotels offering about 250 beds. Schönbüel can sleep more than 100 visitors in the Berghotel Bellevue (30 beds) and a *Touristenlager* with 80 places.

SARNEN (473m) also overlooks its own lake, a beautiful stretch of water from whose northern shore particularly there is a magnificent view south towards the Bernese Alps. Sarnen is the capital of the old Forest Canton of Obwalden, a small town with a charming centre. There is a large and often crowded campsite on the lake shore, some 15 hotels providing accommodation for nearly 500 guests, and 80 holiday chalets and apartments. The town has good shopping facilities, banks, PTT and helpful staff at the tourist information office. An open-air swimming pool is situated next to the campsite, and there's boating on the lake.

KERNS (564m) lies in a sunny position just outside Sarnen and overlooks the valley of the Sarner Aa. The Melchtal road passes through the village. It has an attractive early nineteenth-century church, a few shops, PTT and about 120 hotel beds.

MELCHTAL (890m) has a Benedictine convent and is situated well within the valley on an open meadowland about ten kilometres from Kerns. Above the village a cable-car ascends to Rutialp (1338m) from which a trio of passes lead over the mountains to the Engelbergertal. Melchtal has two hotels with a total of 75 beds.

MELCHSEE-FRUTT (1902m), together with Tannenalp, is the main resort of the valley. With 50 kilometres of footpaths, a wildlife reserve, abundant alpine flora and trout fishing in the lakes, the plateau inhabited by these two small villages attracts those who are content with simple, unsophisticated outdoor recreation. There are a few shops, banking facilities, tourist office and restaurants, and hotels offering standard rooms and *Matratzenlager* accommodation sufficient for 1500 guests. In Tannenalp there is a youth hostel (Berghaus Tannenalp) with 66 beds.

Mountain Huts:
There are no SAC mountain huts within reach of either valley.

Route 74:	Brünig Pass (1008m) - Pilatus Kulm (2067m)

Grade:	3
Distance:	47 kilometres
Height gain:	2407 metres
Height loss:	1423 metres
Time:	4-5 days (total 27-30 hours)
Maps:	L.S. 245 Interlaken, 244 Escholzmatt, 245 Stans 1:50,000

Sponsored by the Obwaldner Kantonalbank in its centenary year the *Brünig-Pilatus Höhenweg* follows a course along the western hills that line the valley of the Sarner Aa. Despite its title this is not a high mountain route as such (the highest point it reaches is the summit of Pilatus), but it is nevertheless one of great character and with a constant shuffling of panoramas. A leaflet is available from various tourist offices in the valley. It includes a map, route profile, a separate sheet of accommodation and transport details, a list of timings and brief description in German. At present there is insufficient accommodation along the way to enable walkers to tackle the complete walk end-to-end without having to depart from the route on one or two sections to find overnight shelter.

The first stage heads north-west from the Brünig Pass to Schönbüel (2011m; 3½-4 hours *accommodation, refreshment*s). Another 1½ hours mostly of descent brings you to a road at Glaubüelen (1565m) from where you can reach Morlialp *(accommodation, refreshments)* in a further 30 minutes. The continuing High Route heads more or less northwards to the Sattel Pass (1589m) and the high point of Miesenegg (1780m) before sloping down to Langis (1432m, 10½ hours from Glaubüelen; *accommodation, refreshments*).

From Langis to the next possibility of accommodation at Lutoldsmatt (1150m) involves another long walk of nearly nine hours, but the final stage to Pilatus Kulm demands less than three hours - time to walk down to Alpnachstad (3 hours) if you'd rather not ride the train.

For further information regarding routes on Pilatus, consult the Vierwaldstättersee section above.

Route 75:	Sarnen (473m) - Wichelsee (460m) - Alpnach (452m)

Grade:	1
Distance:	7 kilometres
Height loss:	21 metres
Time:	1 hour 45 minutes
Map:	L.S. 245 Stans 1:50,000

An easy, undemanding valley walk, this short outing heads downstream towards the open mouth of the valley where Pilatus rises ahead. It uses both footpath and road, traces the shore of a small lake and follows the Sarner Aa on part of its journey to the Alpnacher See.

From the attractive centre of Sarnen head north for a short distance, then go right on a road, then footpath to Chernmatt and Kagiswil station (463m) which you reach in about half an hour. Follow the railway to the Wichelsee lake and take the footpath along its western shore. Beyond the lake cross to the right bank of the river and walk alongside it to a road which eventually recrosses to the left bank and leads directly to Alpnach. Return to Sarnen by train.

Other Walks in the Sarner Aa:
There is no shortage of footpaths to follow in and around the broad and sunny valley of the Sarner Aa. Staff at the tourist offices may be able to provide suggestions, but you are also recommended to study the maps in conjunction with local literature. The Kümmerly & Frey *Wanderbuch, Obwalden* describes fifty or more routes of varying lengths, while the following is but a brief sample.

LUNGERN is idyllically set against its own lake upvalley of Sarnen, and from it a number of fine walks are possible. One popular route climbs to **SCHÖNBÜEL** (2011m) in 4 hours to enjoy spectacular views. This walk could be extended as far as the **BRÜNIG PASS** in a further $2^{1}/_{2}$ hours by way of the Tufengrat and Wileralp.

Another leads west from **SCHÖNBÜEL** (accessible by cable-car from Obsee near Lungern) to the summit of the **BRIENZER ROTHORN** (2349m) in $2^{1}/_{2}$ hours.

At the other end of the valley, a two-day walk from **STANSSTAD** (435m) on the edge of the Vierwaldstättersee to the **BRÜNIG PASS** (1008m) is one way of exploring the Sarner Aa and its villages, its lovely old farms, forests and lakes. Total walking time is about $10^{1}/_{2}$ hours, but since there are lots of opportunities to break away by public transport if you wish, the route can be shortened at will. The route is not a fixed one, for there are various footpaths and narrow roads on both sides of the valley that could be linked. Accommodation is available in a variety of locations.

From **SARNEN** to the minor summit and viewpoint of **JÄNZI** (1737m) west of the town will take $3^{1}/_{2}$ -4 hours by a combination of narrow road, track and footpath. The route is waymarked in yellow *(Wanderweg)* from Sarnen to **CHÄSEREN** (1538m; 3 hours), and from there to the summit with standard red and white *Bergweg* stripes. (A Grade 2 walk.)

The **BRUDER KLAUSENWEG** (Brother Klaus Way) from **FLÜELI** to **STANS** commemorates the local hero, Nicolas von Flue (1417-1487) who was born in the hamlet of Flüeli to the north-east of Sachseln, in whose church he now lies. Having retired as a farmer at the age of fifty, he entered a hermitage in a nearby gorge, became noted for his "sanctity and sense" and was canonised in 1947. This walk goes from his birthplace to **ST NIKLAUSEN, ST ANTONI,** and by way of **ROHRNERBERG** to **STANS** in $4^{1}/_{2}$ hours.

SACHSELN (472m) lies on the eastern shore of the Sarner See. From it an interesting route heads south by way of a quiet road and then a farm track to **ÄLGGIALP** (1650m) above the Klein Melchtal. It then crosses a ridge at **ABGSCHÜTZ** (2222m) to reach **MELCHSEE-FRUTT** (1902m) in 6-$6^{1}/_{2}$ hours. (Grade 3)

Route 76:	Melchsee-Frutt (1902m) - Tannenalp (1974m) - Engstlensee (1850m)

Grade:	2
Distance:	8 kilometres
Height gain:	72 metres
Height loss:	124 metres
Time:	2 hours
Map:	L.S. 255 Sustenpass 1:50,000

An easy but rewarding walk, this recommended route visits the picturesque Engstlensee which lies at the head of the beautiful Gental in the Bernese Alps. The lake spreads across part of the Engstlenalp, described in 1866 by John Tyndall, a Vice-President of the Alpine Club, as "one of the most charming spots in the Alps". Many of its summer visitors would tend to agree with that sentiment.

From Melchsee-Frutt either take the footpath round the southern shore of its lake, the Melchsee, or walk along the narrow service road heading upvalley. The lakeside path rejoins the road at the eastern end and you then follow it as far as Tannenalp (Tannen on the L.S. map). Despite the tarmac it's a pleasant walk between pastures.

Tannenalp is reached in a little over an hour. Bear right near the chapel on a footpath signposted to Engstlenalp, Jochpass and Engelberg. It heads towards the lip of the alp where the ridge subsides to grass and provides a view of the Engstlensee away to the east, with a fine wall of mountains rising above it. Below stretches the deep Gental with a number of waterfalls spraying from the cliffs on the far side, and as the walk progresses, so a superb view is had to the Oberland peaks off to the south-west.

The path crosses pastureland, then rounds a bluff on an easy descending traverse of the crags that form the north wall of the Gental. It slopes down to reach more pastures sliced by streams and rich in flowers in the early summer, then over a footbridge below some cascades, to reach Engstlenalp. (There is a large hotel here with *Matratzenlager* accommodation, and a Postbus halt for Meiringen.) Cross Engstlenalp to the hotel, and take the continuing path behind it which leads in 10 minutes to the Engstlensee.

Allow 2 hours for the return to Melchsee-Frutt by the same path.

Note: Two recommended routes lead downvalley from Engstlenalp and are worth considering if you plan to visit Meiringen. The first is an easy valley walk of $1^1/2$ hours to the hamlet of Schwarzental which has Postbus connection with Innertkirchen and Meiringen. The path begins on the south side of the road near Hotel Engstlenalp and remains on the left bank of the Gentalwasser almost as far as Schwarzental.

The second route is much longer (16 kilometres, $4^1/2$ -5 hours). It takes a belvedere course along the western hillside and passes through several alps before reaching the small village of Reuti above Meiringen. A steep path descends to the valley, while an alternative option would be to ride a cable-car.

Both these routes (and others) are described in full in the guidebook *The Bernese Alps*, published by Cicerone Press.

Route 77:	Melchsee-Frutt (1902m) - Engstlenalp (1834m) - Jochpass (2207m) - Engelberg (1002m)
Grade:	3
Distance:	21 kilometres
Height gain:	377 metres
Height loss:	1329 metres
Time:	6-6$^1/2$ hours
Maps:	L.S. 255 Sustenpass and 245 Stans 1:50,000

This is one of the classic walks of the region which passes through a landscape of lovely views devalued only by an over-abundance of mechanical lifts above Engelberg.

Follow route 76 as far as the Engstlensee (2 hours) and continue along the northern shore of the lake, veering left when the trail forks. (The alternative path goes to a chair-lift which also serves the Jochpass.) The trail climbs in zig-zags to gain height, then eases for a more gentle approach to the pass which is reached in a little over an hour from the

The farm/restaurant of Stäfeli above Engelberg

lake.

The Jochpass is adorned by a cluster of buildings and mechanical aids. There is a Berghotel here with *Matratzenlager* accommodation, and another chair-lift whose route you now follow down towards the Trübsee to the north. On the descent you gain a view of the shining, glacier-draped Titlis to the south-east. At the foot of the slope bear right and walk around the lake shore on a service road towards the Hotel Trübsee (1796m) seen on the far side. The hotel is located at the middle station of the Titlis cableway. Just to the left of the building the continuing path begins a steep zig-zag descent of the Gerschniberg, reaches Gerschnialp (otherwise known as Vorder Stafel; 1257m; *accommodation, refreshments*) and there the way divides. To the left a service road winds down to Engelberg; straight ahead a path goes through woodland and descends to Engelberg by way of Banklialp.

Engelberg has plenty of accommodation and a superb campsite a short distance upvalley. For full details of the resort's facilities consult the Engelbergertal section below.

Route 78:	Melchsee-Frutt (1902m) - Melchtal (890m) - Sachseln (472m)

Grade:	2
Distance:	17 kilometres
Height loss:	1430 metres
Time:	4$\frac{1}{2}$ -5 hours
Maps:	L.S. 255 Sustenpass and 245 Stans 1:50,000

A long downhill walk to the lake shore of the Sarner See, this is a route for those who may have spent time exploring the Melchsee plateau and wish to make a slow exit to the "outside world". It includes a small amount of road walking, but the road is not a busy one.

Start the walk at the western end of the Melchsee on a trail heading north-west that passes between two small pools, soon to reach the alp of Teufiboden (1886m). Beyond there descend to the road, but soon break away from it again, cross the Cheselenbach stream to its left bank and continue down to Stockalp (1075m 1 hour 45 mins). It is possible to catch a Postbus from here to Sarnen.

Follow the road downhill for about 2 kilometres, then leave it on a footpath to the left, heading parallel to the road but then crossing the stream once more to its left bank. If you wish to visit Melchtal (890m; 2 hours 45 mins, *accommodation, refreshments*) you will have to recross to the right bank just south of the village; otherwise continue ahead alongside the stream passing Buel and Sage and down to Hinter Teufibach where the valley begins to curve leftwards. Now take the upper of two trails, cross a tributary stream and enter forest. The continuing path maintains a steady course to Ranft (762m; 4 hours) where study of the map shows a choice of tracks and narrow roads leading down to the lakeside at Sachseln.

Other Walks in the Melchtal:
The above routes provide little more than a sample of the many walks to be had in and from the Melchtal. That there are plenty of options available will be evident from a study of the map. Meanwhile the following suggestions are worth considering.

South of **MELCHSEE-FRUTT** a path climbs beneath a chair-lift to **BALMEREGG** (2255m), bears right and traverses south-westward (fine views of the Wetterhorn) to **PLANPLATTEN** (2186m), then makes a long descending loop of the hillside bowl of Magisalp to reach **KÄSERSTATT** (1831m) after about 3¹/₂ hours (Grade 2). Käserstatt is linked by cable-car with the sun-trap of Hasliberg above Meiringen.

A moderate route of about 2¹/₂ hours (Grade 3) goes from **MELCHSEE-FRUTT** to **ÄLGGIALP** (1650m), Switzerland's geographical centre. It heads first to the **BLAUSEE** tarn, west of Melchsee-Frutt, crosses the northern ridge of the Hochstollen at **ABGSCHÜTZ** (2222m) in less than 1¹/₂ hours, then steers roughly northward above the Seefeld tarn before descending to Älggialp. From here trails lead either to the Klein Melchtal, or via Bachegg (1867m) to Stockalp below Melchsee-Frutt.

From **MELCHTAL** to **ENGELBERG** by way of the **STOREGG PASS** (1742m) is a fine Grade 3 walk of about 6 hours (possible to shorten it by a little over an hour by riding the cable-car to Rütialp). An alternative crossing (via the 2171 metre **JUCHLI PASS**) would take 7-7¹/₂ hours.

ENGELBERGERTAL

Position:	**South of Stans and east of the Melchtal.**
Maps:	**L.S. 245 Stans 1:50,000**
	L.S. 255 Sustenpass 1:50,000
Base:	**Engelberg (1002m)**
Tourist	
Information:	**Verkëhrsverein, 6390 Engelberg (Tel: 041 9411 61)**

Overlooked by the great ice-domed Titlis (3238m) the Engelbergertal provides a justifiably popular centre for mountain holidays in winter and summer alike - as it has for decades. A century ago Engelberg, its main resort, was said by Baedeker to be "Crowded in summer, advisable to write beforehand for rooms". It is still a busy place, but the number of its hotels and apartments has expanded to keep pace with demand and most of its visitors are funnelled toward specific sites, thereby ignoring the more remote corners of the valley where those in search of peace and a degree of seclusion will not be found wanting.

Henry James described the valley as being "grim, ragged, rather vacuous, but by no means absolutely unbeautiful", and walkers who allow themselves time to explore it properly will agree that it most certainly is not "unbeautiful".

It begins in the embrace of an almost perfect amphitheatre of peaks some way upstream and to the east of Engelberg. Blackenalp, with its small farm and solitary white-walled chapel perched on a bluff, forms a green oasis, an undulating floor to this amphitheatre with huge rock walls soaring to north, east and west. From them streams come chasing in youthful vigour and join forces below the chapel. One of these streams is born below the Surenenpass among a rucked contortion of pasture with two or three small tarns trapped there. Sheep graze the pastures in summer and chamois nose among the screes that bound them.

The Stierenbach (later to become the Engelberger Aa) escapes the amphitheatre at its southern opening, then curves clockwise round

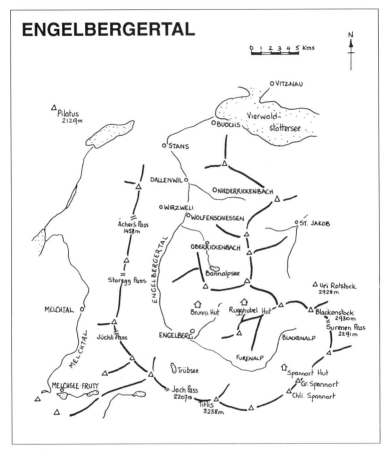

the flanks of the Wissberg. High above to the south-east rise the Spannort peaks, while the Titlis stands as a proud bastion of rock at the south-western bend, its vast walls appearing impossibly steep and unclimbable. Seen from here the mountain does indeed seem impregnable, yet its north-western slopes reveal a weakness discovered long ago. In 1744 it was the first of Switzerland's snow-peaks to be climbed.

Below the Titlis the river is channelled north-westward, at first among avalanche-wrecked forests, then between low-lying meadows until it reaches Engelberg where the direction changes once more and the flow is mostly to the north. A short distance downstream from Engelberg the valley has been squeezed and the road twists in wooded hairpins to overcome the severity of the slope.

Just south of the small resort of Wolfenschiessen the river receives the Sechlisbach tributary which drains a secondary glen to the south-east. Oberrickenbach lies in this glen, and from it a number of cable-cars ascend the surrounding hillsides.

North of Wolfenschiessen the valley runs straight and level, broadening on the approach to Stans with a flood of light and space after the long constrictions of the upper valley. And for the majority of travellers journeying by road or rail to Engelberg, it is from here that the valley properly begins. This is its gateway, for only the hardened mountain walker, for whom high cols form an irresistible lure, may approach from any other direction. (See, for example, Routes 14 and 77.) Such "back country" routes of approach reveal the valley's true splendour in the finest possible manner.

Main Valley Base:

ENGELBERG (1002m) developed around the large Benedictine abbey that was founded about 1120 and named *Mons Angelorum* by Pope Calixtus II, from whose Germanised form Engelberg takes its name. The abbey has been burned and rebuilt several times; it is open to the public (check times) and is worth a visit. The town has all modern resort facilities, and can accommodate some 8000 guests in a variety of hotels, apartments and *Gasthofs*, including several *Matratzenlagers*. A youth hostel (*Jugendherberg*) in the town can sleep 150 and to the south a very well-appointed campsite even has its own indoor swimming pool and sauna. Engelberg lies just 34 kilometres from Lucerne and is accessible from it by train. The N3 Basle-Chiasso motorway passes the mouth of the valley about 20 kilometres away.

Other Accommodation:
Overnight lodgings are available in various forms throughout the valley and on the surrounding hills. Upvalley of Engelberg, for example, the alp building at **BLACKENALP** (1773m) has *Matratzenlager* spaces for 20; **STÄFELI** (1393m), an hour's walk downstream from Blackenalp, can accommodate 42. On the shelf of hillside above and to the north of Stäfeli, **HOBIEL** (1673m) also offers bedspace in a *Matratzenlager*.

High above Engelberg to the south there's the **HOTEL TRÜBSEE** (1796m) easily accessible by cable-car. The Berghotel at the **JOCHPASS** (2207m) above it, and the **PENSION UNTERTRÜBSEE** (1250m) below, each have modestly-priced *Matratzenlager* accommodation.

For full details enquire at the Engelberg tourist office for the *Touristenlager* and Hotel lists.

Downvalley accommodation is to be found in **GRAFENORT** (569m), **OBERRICKENBACH** (894m) and **BANNALP** (1598m) above it, at **WOLFENSCHIESSEN** (511m) and **DALLENWIL** (544m).

Mountain Huts:
The SAC has four huts accessible from the Engelbergertal.

On the eastern side of the valley above Engelberg stands the **BRUNNI HUT** (1860m), easily reached in just 40 minutes from the top station of the Brunni/Ristis cable-car. The hut can sleep 60 people in its dormitories. It is open all-year and with a guardian in permanent residence to provide meals and drinks (tel: 041 9421 70).

The **RUGGHUBEL HUT** (2294m) is found east of the Brunni Hut on the southern slopes of the Ruchstock. Owned by Section Titlis from Stans, it has places for 80 and a guardian from the middle of June until the end of October, during which time meals and drinks are available. The hut is reached in 4$^{1/2}$ hours from Engelberg, or via the Brunni/Ristis cable-car in 2$^{1/2}$ -3 hours (tel: 041 9420 64).

Approached by path in a little under two hours from Stäfeli in the upper reaches of the valley, the **SPANNORT HUT** (1956m) was provided by the Zürich-based Uto Section. It has room for 45 and a guardian during summer weekends who provides meals and drinks (tel: 041 9434 80). This is very much a climber's hut with some fine routes to tackle on assorted rock walls that rise behind it.

There is also the **GRASSEN BIVOUAC HUT** (2650m) perched high above the valley under the south-eastern flanks of the Titlis, but the approach to it lies outside the scope of this walker's guide.

Route 79:	Engelberg (1002m) - Surenen Pass (2291m) - Attinghausen (469m)
Grade:	3
Distance:	26 kilometres
Height gain:	1289 metres
Height loss:	1822 metres
Time:	9-9½ hours
Map:	L.S. 245 Stans and 246 Klausenpass 1:50,000

An epic crossing of the mountains from the Engelbergertal to the valley of the Reuss, this very full-day's journey is the reverse of Route 14 already described, and is highly recommended to all those who delight in long and challenging mountain walks. It's possible to break the walk with an overnight in a *Matratzenlager* in the following places, with times given from Engelberg: Stäfeli (1393m; 2 hours 30 mins), Blackenalp (1773m; 4 hours) and Brüsti (1525m; 7 hours). It is also possible to shorten the walk by about 2 hours by taking a cable-car from Brüsti down to Attinghausen.

From Engelberg walk upvalley, either on the road initially, or alongside the river (south bank on the so-called *Professorenweg*) until there's an opportunity to cross to the opposite bank near the cable-car station towards the head of the valley. A track continues upvalley, curving leftwards and passing the buildings of Alpenrösli (1258m; *refreshments*). Soon after you come to Stäfeli (*accommodation, refreshments).*

Above Stäfeli the track becomes a path which steadily rises towards a fine waterfall (Stauber). It climbs along the left-hand side of this to enter a short upper region of the valley, and through this to enter Blackenalp (1773m; 4 hours; *accommodation, refreshments*) with its small white chapel and farm, and a magnificent backdrop of mountain walls forming a superb amphitheatre.

Pass the chapel and the alp building and continue north-westwards, rising steeply in places over a rough pastureland. In a little under 1¹/₂ hours from Blackenalp you reach the Surenen Pass (2291m) with its glorious views. Descend across screes on the eastern side, and when you come to a path junction, take the left fork which leads along a grassy ridge (Grat) affording more fine views, this time leftwards steeply down to the Urnersee. At the end of the Grat ridge the way veers to the right and descends, in places with cable support, and brings you to the hamlet of chalets that is Brüsti (1525m 7 hours). Two of the chalets offer accommodation. There is also a cable-car which leads from here down to Attinghausen in two stages.

The continuing path passes the cable-car station, switchbacks south, then veers left again and descends steeply through woods to the middle station of the cableway, and goes down steeply once more to emerge at Attinghausen near a couple of hotels, one of which has *Matratzenlager* accommodation. (Altdorf is another 2 kilometres away across the valley.)

Route 80:	Engelberg (Fürenalp; 1840m) - Blackenalp (1773m) - Engelberg (1002m)
Grade:	2
Distance:	16 kilometres
Height loss:	840 metres
Height gain:	143 metres
Time:	4¹/₂ -5 hours
Map:	L.S. 245 Stans 1:50,000

One of the less-demanding ways to visit the head of the Surenental (the upper reaches of the Engelbergertal) is to ride the cable-car to Fürenalp and to follow a very pleasant path to Blackenalp before returning downvalley to Engelberg. Views are delightful all the way: first to the Titlis, then the pinnacles of the Gross and Klein Spannort,

Titlis from the path to Blackenalp

the brazen cliffs of the Schlössberg and lastly looking up at the great amphitheatre of peaks encircling Blackenalp. There are lively streams and waterfalls along the way, flower-rich meadows, alp hamlets, farms that double as restaurants and a lovely little chapel.

The valley station of the Fürenalp cable-car is located about 5 kilometres upstream of Engelberg at Herrenrüti-boden (1084m) where there is a large parking area.

Leaving the upper cable-car station at Fürenalp (a splendid observation point) take the obvious footpath heading east and signposted to Aussenebnet, Stauber and Alpenrösli. From the outset there are stunning views to enjoy, while the high pastures through which the path wanders are extravagant with flowers in summer. The path slopes easily down the hillside on the flanks of the Wissberg before dropping more steeply towards the alp hamlet of Aussenebnet, which is marked as Usser Abnet (1670m) on the map. The trail passes above the hamlet at a more gentle angle, now heading north-east, and soon passing to the left of Alp Hobiel (1673m) which offers accommodation and refreshments.

Continuing, reach a junction of trails in full view of the Stauber waterfall (1630m). Take the path which climbs north-eastwards alongside a minor stream and this eventually brings you to Blackenalp (1¹/₂ hours). Refreshments are available at the alp building.

Return downvalley by the same path to the Stauber waterfall, and from there remain on the descending trail which leads through the valley on its right-hand flank. This brings you to Stäfeli (1393m; 2¹/₂ hours; *refreshments*), and 30 minutes later to Alpenrösli (1258m; *refreshments*) where there is a choice of routes. Either follow the track along the north bank of the river until you come to the road, which you follow back to Engelberg, or cross the river here and walk along the continuing footpath until it returns you to the right bank where you rejoin the main route to Engelberg.

Route 81:	**Engelberg (Fürenalp; 1840m) - Dagenstal (1587m) - Ober Zieblen (1631m) - Engelberg (1002m)**

Grade:	**2-3**
Distance:	**6.5 kilometres**
Height gain:	**116 metres**
Height loss:	**838 metres**
Time:	**2-2¹/₂ hours**
Map:	**L.S. 245 Stans 1:50,000**

Almost every valley has its high route, a belvedere trail that traverses one of the flanking hillsides at mid-height. This walk is part of the Engelbergertal's high route, although it is not known as such. Following heavy rain caution is advised, especially on the steep descent from Ober Zieblen.

From the Fürenalp cable-car station bear left on the trail signposted to Dagenstal, Ober Zieblen and Engelberg. It heads north-westward along the steep hillside with fine views across the valley to the Titlis, and soon arrives at the alp buildings of Vorder Füren (1804m). Continuing in the same direction, and losing height all the time, you come to a path junction. Take the right-hand option which cuts into the mouth of the shallow Dagenstal, and crossing the stream which issues from it reach another alp about 40 minutes after leaving Fürenalp.

The trail passes the alp buildings, rises to round a grassy shoulder of hillside and before long takes you into the upper portion of forest that clothes the slopes of the mountain. In places the path is quite narrow. It reaches a high point of 1703 metres (Rinder Alp), then undulates, still among trees, to reach Ober Zieblen (1631m 1½ hours). Once again there is a junction of trails. Bear left and descend steeply, crossing beneath a farm hoist and, when you reach the valley floor, bear right and walk along a service road into Engelberg.

Route 82:	Engelberg (1002m) - Ober Zieblen (1631m) - Dagenstal (1587m) - Engelberg

Grade:	**3**
Distance:	**10 kilometres**
Height gain/loss:	**703 metres**
Time:	**5½ hours**
Map:	**L.S. 245 Stans 1:50,000**

The high route described in Route 81 extends into the glen of the Barenbach which cuts into the mountains north-east of Engelberg. The following walk explores that section of the route, retraces part of the trail already described, then returns into the valley by an alternative path. It's a splendid walk, but is more strenuous than the preceding route on account of the steep climb out of Horbis. Beyond Horbis (about 50 minutes from Engelberg) there are no further opportunities for refreshment, so take food and drink with you.

Walk out of Engelberg past the abbey (Kloster) and follow a minor road which heads left up into the glen of the Barenbach following its stream. The road is signposted to Hinter Horbis and End der Welt. As you come to a tarn with a weir at its southern end, seen on the left of the road, a track leads away ahead to the right. This offers

The chapel at End der Velt, Engelberg

an alternative to the surfaced road and is kinder to your feet. In about 50 minutes come to Horbis with its cluster of buildings, including an attractive chapel and a restaurant. Take the footpath which branches off to the right behind the restaurant, signposted to Ober Zieblen.

It climbs steeply among trees, then comes to a long narrow grass strip dividing the forest. The way zig-zags up it, gaining height at a moderate gradient. Halfway up the slope the way forks. The left branch goes to Furggialp, while the right branch is the one to take for Ober Zieblen. Continue to gain height, cross a stream-bed and zig-zag through more forest, emerging at a single hut (Zieblenzof; 1456m; $2^{1}/2$ hours) at the foot of a very steep meadow. The way now heads up the left-hand edge of the meadow, and near the top bears right to cross it, passes through more trees and slopes up another open pasture to reach the farm building of Ober Zieblen (1631m; 2 hours 50 mins).

There is a very fine view of the Titlis from here. Ignoring the path which drops to the right, continue ahead among trees high above the valley. There are two or three avalanche chutes and gullies to cross, but these are short steps only and the way leads on, rising and falling as it does. When you come out of the trees views are spectacular. About 50 minutes from Ober Zieblen come to the alp at the opening of the Dagenstal (1587m).

Bear right on a descending path signposted to Vorder Stalden and Engelberg. This soon leads to two buildings at Undrist Stafel. Although it is still waymarked, the trail from here is a little obscure. Descend directly to a pylon where you will see below and a little to the right, a signpost on a junction of paths. Go down to this and bear right on the descending path to Engelberg. This takes you across pastures and through woodlands, eventually leading into the valley at a road where you turn right to complete the walk back to Engelberg.

Route 83:	Engelberg (1002m) - Ober Zieblen (1631m) - Fürenalp (1840m) - Stauber (1630m) - Engelberg

Grade:	3
Distance:	21 kilometres
Height gain/loss:	838 metres
Time:	$7^{1}/_{2}$ -8 hours
Map:	L.S. 245 Stans 1:50,000

By combining much of the three previously described walks, the full high belvedere route above the Engelbergertal can be achieved. It's a full day's walk, but there are several refreshment stops along the way, and also opportunities for breaking the journey with an overnight spent in a secluded *Matratzenlager* if desired.

The first stage follows the trail described in Route 82 from Engelberg as far as the alp in the mouth of the Dagenstal (1587m). Continue on the high path which skirts the entrance to the glen, crosses the stream and then heads round the hillside to Fürenalp (Route 81 in reverse). Fürenalp (1840m; 4 hours 15 mins) provides an opportunity for refreshment - also cable-car descent to the valley if needed.

From here follow the path outlined as far as the Stauber waterfall

193

(1630m; 5 hours 15 mins) as in Route 80, but instead of continuing up to Blackenalp, bear right and wander downvalley (also described in Route 80) passing Stäfeli *(accommodation, refreshments)* and Alpenrösli *(refreshments)*, all the way back to Engelberg. A fine day out.

Route 84:	Engelberg (1002m) - Stäfeli (1393m) - Spannort Hut (1956m)

Grade:	3
Distance:	10 kilometres
Height gain:	954 metres
Time:	4 hours
Map:	L.S. 245 Stans 1:50,000

As mentioned in the introductory section, this climber's hut is situated high above the upper valley on the slopes of the Spannort peaks. It can accommodate 45 in its dormitories and there's a guardian on the premises usually during summer weekends.

Walk upvalley from Engelberg, preferably along the *Professorenweg* which follows the south bank of the river. Beyond the campsite cross to the north side and continue upvalley, now along the road, then track, as far as Stäfeli (1393m), a farm building that doubles as a restaurant and also has *Matratzenlager* accommodation. Cross the stream here on a marked path. It soon forks. Take the right-hand trail and begin to climb steeply heading east. The path leads directly to the hut, reached in a little under two hours from Stäfeli.

Route 85:	Engelberg (1002m) - Trübsee (1764m) - Unter Trübsee (1300m) - Engelberg

Grade:	2-3
Distance:	12 kilometres
Height gain/loss:	769 metres
Time:	4-4^{1}/2 hours
Map:	L.S. 245 Stans 1:50,000

South of Engelberg the mountainside rises in well-defined steps to the Titlis. The first step, separated from the valley floor by a wall of forest, is shared by the Gerschnialp and Unter Trübsee. Mechanical lifts rather clutter the slopes and provide ease of access to great throngs of visitors. The next step contains the lake of Trübsee with its surfaced circular walk, its hotel, cable-car to the Klein Titlis (easy walk from there to the summit of the Titlis itself for an incredible panorama of high mountains), and a chair-lift to the Jochpass. It's not a place to find peace and solitude, but it does have a remarkable view up to the glaciers and snowfields of the Titlis.

This walk climbs to the upper Trübsee plateau, skirts the lake, then descends over pastureland via the lower step back to the valley again.

From the railway station take the footpath heading south-east across to the river, then over this go up to Banklialp. A continuing footpath climbs among trees (the Gerschniwald), switchbacking to ease the ascent, and emerges onto the shelf of hillside at Vorder Stafel (1257m; 1 hour; *refreshments*). At a junction of trails take the upper path heading south for the steepening hillside and begin the long zig-zag ascent towards Hotel Trübsee. Near the top of the climb cable-cars pass annoyingly overhead.

Reach the upper Trübsee plateau next to the hotel and cable-car station in about 2¹/₂ hours. Walk ahead to the left-hand end of the lake, pass round to the far side and continue to the chair-lift station. From here ignore the path which climbs towards the Jochpass and instead head north-west along a trail that continues beyond the end of the lake and keeps to the left of a stream (the Trüebenbach). The path descends alongside it, crosses to the right bank and then drops down to Unter Trübsee *(refreshments)*. From here a choice of routes lead down to Engelberg, one of which is by service road.

Route 86:	Engelberg (1002m) - Jochpass (2207m) - Engstlenalp (1834m)

Grade:	3
Distance:	13 kilometres
Height gain:	1205 metres
Height loss:	373 metres
Time:	4$^{1}/_{2}$ -5 hours
Maps:	L.S. 245 Stans and 255 Sustenpass 1:50,000

One of the stages of the classic alpine traverse known as the Alpine Pass Route crosses the Jochpass on its way from Engelberg to Meiringen - a very long stage of 9$^{1}/_{2}$ hours. Though only part of that lengthy stage, this particular walk is a strenuous one as far as the pass, but the descent is kind to tired legs, and at the end of the day there's accommodation waiting at Hotel Engstlenalp (it has *Matratzenlager* as well as standard rooms) with beautiful views along the Gental to the Wetterhorn's coronet of peaks. (The walk was described in the reverse direction from Melchsee-Frutt in the Melchtal and Sarner Aa section.)

Follow directions for Route 85 as far as the chair-lift station at Trübsee (about 2 hours 50 mins). Just before the chair-lift a path breaks away to the left. This is the one to take. It climbs for about an hour without difficulty, although it's an eroded trail and the chair-lift whirrs constantly overhead. (Look out for marmots along this path.)

Arriving at the Jochpass in about 3 hours 50 minutes you will find a clutter of buildings, including a Berghaus offering accommodation and refreshments. The continuing path on the far side of the pass heads south-westward beneath yet another chair-lift. Fortunately you soon lose this and can enjoy lovely views of the Engstlensee below, and the Wetterhorn ahead, without the mechanical distraction.

The descending trail eases down to the Engstlensee, then cuts across meadowland to reach the large Hotel Engstlenalp. This stands at the head of a road served by Postbus through the Gental to Innertkirchen, and then on to Meiringen, for those whose need is to move further west.

Note: For downvalley walks from Engstlenalp, refer to the guide *The Bernese Alps*. For full description of the Alpine Pass Route (Sargans to Montreux), see the guidebook devoted to it. Both books are published by Cicerone Press.

Route 87:	Engelberg (1002m) - Juchli Pass (2171m) - Melchtal (890m)

Grade:	3
Distance:	11 kilometres
Height gain:	1169 metres
Height loss:	1281 metres
Time:	6¹/₂ -7 hours
Map:	L.S. 245 Stans 1:50,000

The Juchli Pass is situated to the west of Engelberg in the high ridge linking the peaks of Huetstock with that of the Nünalphorn, part of the extensive ridge system which divides the Melchtal from the Engelbergertal. Although this crossing is somewhat strenuous, it has a reputation for being scenically attractive and dramatic in places. Chamois are frequently seen in the region of the pass, and far views of big mountains contrast with the lesser - but by no means unlovely - hills of the north. The Melchtal has its own special beauty, and for details of accommodation and other walking routes there, consult the Melchtal and Sarner Aa section above.

The walk begins either by taking the service road which winds up the southern hillside through Unter Trübsee and on to Arni Wang (Wanghütte, 1333m), or by footpath from the western end of Engelberg's small tarn. This path heads up through Ortigen and by a forest trail to reach the Wanghütte in about 1¹/₂ hours. A short track continues from here to Haltenhütte (1340m) where you take the footpath heading west beside the Arnibach and climbing steeply up the flanks of the Nünalphorn (2384m).

The Juchli Pass is reached in a little over 4 hours from the start, and the deep Melchtal lies far below to the west. The descent to it is steep and taxing. It leads by way of Nünalp (2130m), 10 minutes from the pass, then via the alp buildings of Stäfeli (1800m), Stock (1515m) and Turren (1229m), this last being reached 2 hours below the Juchli Pass. Melchtal village is just half an hour's walk from here, first through forest then across open pastures.

Note: A less-demanding route linking the two valleys is by way of the Storegg Pass (1742m) which lies to the north of the Juchli Pass, on the far side of the Widderfeld Stock. This walk will require about 6 hours to complete. (Grade 3)

Route 88:	Engelberg (Brunni/Ristis; 1606m) - Brunni Hut (1860m)

Grade:	**2-3**
Distance:	**1.5 kilometres**
Height gain:	**254 metres**
Time:	**40 minutes**
Map:	**L.S. 245 Stans 1:50,000**

Commanding a delightful panorama of the Engelberger mountains the Brunni Hut may be reached by a walk of $2^{1}/_{2}$-3 hours, or by a much shorter approach using the Brunni cable-car, thus making it a popular place with day visitors. This is the route given here.

Ride the Engelberg-Brunni cableway north of the town to Ristis (1606m) where refreshments are available. The path to the hut begins here and is signposted. It leads directly up the mountainside, with many temptations to stop along the way to enjoy the views that seem to grow more expansive as you gain height. So reach the hut, with its lovely views from the terrace. A guardian is in permanent residence, so meals and drinks are available. It can accommodate 60.

Route 89:	Engelberg (Brunni/Ristis; 1606m) - Rugghubel Hut (2294m)

Grade:	**3**
Distance:	**6 kilometres**
Height gain:	**688 metres**

Time:	2¹/₂ -3 hours
Map:	L.S 245 Stans 1:50,000

The Rugghubel Hut stands upon the slopes of the Engelberger Rotstock in the midst of an amphitheatre of peaks to the east of the Brunni Hut. Below it the Griessental falls to the main valley, steep cliffs that plunge to forest and pasture. Above the hut a crossing of the Rot Grätli, the western ridge of the Rotstock, leads to the Grosstal which drains through Isenthal into the Urnersee - the southern finger of the Vierwaldstättersee.

The hut itself is owned by the Stans-based Titlis Section of the Swiss Alpine Club. It's a sturdy-looking building that can accommodate 80 people. Meals and drinks are available from mid-June to the end of October when the guardian is on duty.

Leaving the upper station of the Engelberg-Brunni cable-car walk along the track which heads north-eastward to Rigidalstafel (1745m), an alp high above the valley. (A path rises to this point in 2¹/₂ hours from Engelberg.) Continue beyond the alp on a long rising traverse of mountainside above grey cliff bands, the Griessental now far below. In a scanty pasture at the head of the valley are the alp buildings of Planggenstafel. The trail passes below these heading almost due east, still rising steadily, and finally reaches the hut.

Note: To walk all the way from Engelberg takes 4-4¹/₂ hours. To return to the cable-car station from the hut, allow about 1 hour 40m.

Route 90:	Engelberg (Brunni/Ristis; 1606m) - Oberrickenbach (894m) -Niederrickenbach (1158m)
Grade:	3
Distance:	20 kilometres
Height gain:	834 metres
Height loss:	1236 metres
Time:	6-6¹/₂ hours
Map:	L.S. 245 Stans 1:50,000

This route is publicised locally as the *Benediktusweg*, a high path leading north along the valley's eastern hillsides, linking a number of alps and giving an opportunity for walkers to glimpse some of the delights of the countryside around the two small resorts of Oberrickenbach and Niederrickenbach. A leaflet outlining the route, with a map and route profile, is available from Engelberg's tourist office. It suggests starting the walk by using the Engelberg-Brunni cable-car, and at the end of the trek taking cable-car from Niederrickenbach down to Dallenwil in the valley. Refreshments are available at several places along the way, and it's also possible to divide the route into two short stages by spending a night in Oberrickenbach.

The walk begins by heading north-west from Ristis (the upper station of the Brunni cableway), descending a little to Hinter Sack and Chruteren (1551m), then climbing over the spur of Stock (1730m 50 mins). A steady descent takes the continuing path through Alp Stafel and straight ahead at a trail junction to reach Walenalp (1671m $1^{1}/_{2}$ hours). Walenalp is on the western flank of the Walenstocke, beyond which lies the basin of Oberrickenbach, while hidden above it to the south is the little reservoir of Bannalpsee.

Oberrickenbach is reached in a little over three hours from Ristis. It has *Gasthaus* and *Matratzenlager* accommodation. A road heads down from here to Wolfenschiessen, while several cableways lace the surrounding hillsides.

The *Benediktusweg* continues, now heading north-west and rising to Brandlen (1188m), then after reaching a high point of 1351 metres (Plütschgen) a descent begins that will go through the Steinalperwald, rising once more to the Alpboden Brücke and then sloping down for 2 kilometres into Niederrickenbach (3 hours from Oberrickenbach; 6-$6^{1}/_{2}$ hours from Ristis). Accommodation is available here in a hotel with beds and *Matratzenlager*.

Other Walks in and from the Engelbergertal:

Numerous other walks are possible in and around the valley. The map serves as inspiration, but there is also a *Wanderkarte* on sale locally at a scale of 1:25,000 with plenty of recommendations marked upon it, and with outline notes on the reverse. Anyone planning a walking holiday based in Engelberg would be advised to buy a copy. The tourist office also sells a panoramic map *(Panoramakarte)* with notes on the reverse suggesting various walks in the surrounding area. In addition the following outline routes are offered.

A day's walk leads upvalley from **ENGELBERG** along the southern mountainside to **HOHFAD** (1450m) and **BODMEN** (1323m), before descending into the valley at **HERRENRÜTI** ($3^{1}/_{2}$ hours) and returning by a gentle valley path.

A valley walk of 2-$2^{1}/_{2}$ hours takes you downstream from **ENGELBERG** through the river's gorge to **OBERMATT** and **GRAFENORT**. A trail follows the Engelberger Aa all the way; first on the left bank until just before reaching Obermatt, then on the right bank for a further 2 kilometres (the railway for company) before returning to the left bank for the final stretch to Grafenort (accommodation in a *Gasthaus*).

From **GRAFENORT** (569m) a four-hour walk leads up the western hillside (first downstream to Gross Fallenbach) to **DIEGISBALM** (1000m), **WISSIFLUE** (1144m) and the hamlet of **WIRZWELI** (1222m; accommodation in *Gasthaus* and *Matratzenlager*). Wirzweli is connected with Dallenwil in the valley by cable-car, and by a narrow tortuous road.

An easy $2^{1}/_{2}$ -hour walk leads from **WIRZWELI** to **STANS** (451m), from where trains lead to Lucerne and Engelberg.

On the eastern side of the valley, a pleasant cross-country route links **NIEDERRICKENBACH** with the historic boathouse/ferry point of **TREIB** on the Urnersee opposite Brunnen (see Vierwaldstättersee section). This $5^{1}/_{2}$ hour walk heads roughly north-east, starting at 1162 metres, rising to **BARENFÄLLEN** at 1580 metres, then descending to **EMMETTEN** (774m) in about $3^{1}/_{2}$ hours. From here a trail heads mostly through forest for a little under 2 hours to reach **TREIB**. Lake steamers regularly call at this point.

APPENDIX A
Useful Addresses

1: Tourist Information Offices - other than those mentioned elsewhere with regard to specific bases:

Swiss National Tourist Office

Swiss Centre
Swiss Court
London W1V 8EE

250 Stockton Street
San Francisco
CA 94108

104 South Michigan Avenue
Chicago
Il 60603
M5L 1E8

Commerce Court
Toronto
Ontario

608 Fifth Avenue
New York
NY 10020

Central Switzerland Tourist Assn.
Alpenstrasse 1
CH 6002 Lucerne
Switzerland

2: Useful Addresses in Switzerland:

Schweizer Hotelier-Verein
(Swiss Hotel Association)
Monbijoustrasse 130
CH 3001 Bern

Schweizer Alpen Club
(Swiss Alpine Club)
Helvetiaplatz 4
CH 3005 Bern

Schweizerischer Camping und Caravanning-Verband
(Swiss Camping & Caravanning Association)
Habsburgerstrasse 35
CH 6004 Lucerne

Verband Schweizer Camping
(Swiss Camping Association)
Im Sydefädeli 40
CH 8037 Zürich

Schweizerischer Bund für Jugendherbergen
(Swiss Youth Hostels Association)
Postfach 3229
CH 3001 Bern 22

Touring Club der Schweiz
*(Swiss motoring organisation
    affiliated to the AA)*
Rue Pierre-Fatio 9
Geneva

Automobil-Club der Schweiz
(affiliated to the RAC)
Wasserwerkgasse 39
CH 3001 Bern

3: Map Suppliers:
Cordee (Mail Order)
3a De Montfort Street
Leicester LE1 7HD

Edward Stanford Ltd
12-14 Long Acre
London WC2E 9LP

The Map Shop
15 High Street
Upton-upon-Severn
Worcs WR8 0HJ

Rand McNally Map Store
10 East 53rd Street
New York
NY 10022

APPENDIX B
Glossary

The following glossary lists a few words likely to be found on maps, in village streets or in foreign-language tourist information leaflets.

German	English	German	English
Abend	evening	Garni	hotel with meals optional
Abfahrt	start, departure or descent	Gasthaus or	inn or guest
Abhang	slope	Gasthof	house
Alp	alp or high pasture	Gaststube	common room
Alpenblume	alpine flower	Gefärhlich	dangerous
Alpenverein	alpine club	Gemse	chamois
Alphütte	mountain hut	Geröllhalde	scree
Auskunft	information	Gipfel	summit, peak
Aussichtspunkt	viewpoint	Gletscher	glacier
		Gletscherspalte	crevasse
Bach	stream	Gondelbahn	gondola lift
Bäckerei	bakery	Grat	ridge
Bahnhof	railway station	Grüetzi	greetings
Berg	mountain		
Bergführer	mountain guide	Haltestelle	bus stop
Berggasthaus	mountain inn	Heilbad	spa, hot springs
Bergpass	pass	Hirsch	red deer
Bergschrund	crevasse between rock wall & glacier	Hoch	high
		Höhe	height
Bergsteiger	mountaineer	Höhenweg	high route
Bergwanderer	mountain walker	Horn	horn, peak
Bergweg	mountain path	Hügel	hill
Blatt	map sheet	Hütte	mountain hut
Brücke	bridge		
		Jugendherberge	youth hostel
Dorf	village		
Drahtseilbahn	cable-car	Kamm	crest or ridge
		Kapelle	chapel
Ebene	plain	Karte	map
		Kirche	church
Feldweg	meadowland path	Klamm	gorge
Fels	rock wall or slope	Klumme	combe or small valley
Fereinwohnung	holiday apartment		
Fussweg	footpath		

German	English	German	English
Landschaft	landscape	Seeli	small tarn
Lawine	avalanche	Seil	rope
Lebensmittel	grocery	Seilbahn	cable-car
Leicht	easy	Sesselbahn	chair-lift
Links	left (direction)	Stausee	reservoir
		Steigeisen	crampons
Matratzenlager	dormitory	Steinmann	cairn
Milcherei	dairy	Steinschlag	falling rock
Moräne	moraine	Stunde(n)	hour(s)
Murmeltier	marmot	Sud	south
Nebel	fog, low cloud, mist	Tal	valley
Nord	north	Tobel	wooded ravine
Ober	upper	Touristenlager	dormitory, tourist accommodation
Ost	east		
Pass	pass	Über	via or over
Pension	simple hotel	Unfall	accident
Pfad	path	Unterkunft	accommodation
Pickel	ice axe	Verkehrsbüro/	
Quelle	spring (water)	Verkehrsverein	tourist office
Rechts	right	Wald	forest
Reh	roe deer	Wanderweg	footpath
Reiseburo	travel office	Wasser	water
Rucksack	rucksack	Weide	pasture
Sattel	saddle, pass	West	west
Schlafraum	bedroom	Wildbach	torrent
Schloss	castle		
Schlucht	gorge	Zeltplatz	campsite
Schnee	snow	Zimmer	bedroom
See	lake, tarn	- frei	vacancies
		Zurück	return

BIBLIOGRAPHY

1: General Tourist Guides
There are many general tourist guides to Switzerland, but perhaps the best and
most comprehensive is -
Blue Guide to Switzerland by Ian Robertson (A. & C.Black, London. W.W.Norton,
New York - latest edition 1991).
See also *Off the Beaten Track - Switzerland,* and *The Visitor's Guide to Switzerland* by
John Marshall (both by Moorland Publishing Co., Ashbourne, in 1989 and 1990
respectively).

2: Mountains and Mountaineering

Surprisingly few mountaineering books can be found in English that devote much space to the Central Swiss Alps. The activities of a few pioneers are briefly recorded in historical surveys, but little up-to-date. The following climbers' guides are still available -

Central Switzerland by Jeremy O.Talbot (West Col Productions, Goring, 1969) covers the region contained within an area bounded by the Susten, Grimsel and Furka Passes, and the Reuss valley.

Engelhörner and Salbitschijen by Jeremy O.Talbot (West Col Productions, Goring, 1968).

3: Walking

Again, very little has appeared in English of interest to walkers visiting the area covered by this guide. Exceptions are as follows -

Alpine Pass Route by Kev Reynolds (Cicerone Press, Milnthorpe, 1990) is a guide to the classic long-distance walk which traverses country covered by the present guidebook, and *Classic Walks in the Alps* by Kev Reynolds (Oxford Illustrated Press, Sparkford, 1991) also includes an account of that walk.

Footloose in the Swiss Alps by William Reifsnyder (Sierra Club, San Francisco, 1979 - 2nd edition) includes details of a long walk which passes through the region from Engstlenalp to the Muotatal.

Six foreign-language guidebooks for walkers, published in German by Kümmerly & Frey of Bern, cover the region described in this present guide. They are - *Nidwalden, Obwalden, Uri, Vierwaldstättersee, Luzern Pilatus,* and *Schweiz.*

4: Mountain Flowers

The Alpine Flowers of Britain and Europe by Christopher Grey-Wilson and Marjorie Blamey (Collins, London, 1979) is a very useful pocket identification book.

Mountain Flowers by Anthony Huxley (Blandford Press, London, 1967) is another fine book to help identify species found in the areas covered by this guide. Illustrations are by Daphne Barry and Mary Grierson.

ROUTE INDEX

Route		Grade	Time	Page
1	Rigi Kulm-Vitznau	1-2	2^1/$_2$ -3 hrs	44
2	Vitznau-Kaltbad-Rigi Kulm	2	3 hrs 45 mins	46
3	Vitznau-Unterstetten-Rigi Kulm	2-3	3^1/$_2$ hrs	46
4	Vitznau-Rigi Scheidegg	2-3	3^1/$_2$ -4 hrs	47
5	Rütli-Seelisberg-Bauen-Flüelen	1-2	6-6^1/$_2$ hrs	50
6	Flüelen-Sisikon-Morschach-Brunnen	1-2	5 hrs	52
7	Brunnen-Morschach	1	1 hr 15 mins	54
8	Brunnen-Morschach-Stoos	2	3-3^1/$_2$ hrs	55
9	Brunnen-Morschach-Sisikon	1-2	3 hrs	56

Route		Grade	Time	Page
10	Brunnen-Schranggigen-Ranggen-Lauerz	2	$3^{1}/_2$ hrs	57
11	Altdorf-Eggberge	2-3	3 hrs	58
12	Altdorf (Gitschenberg)-Seedorf	2	$3^{1}/_2$ hrs	59
13	Altdorf (Gitschenberg)-Brüsti	3	$4-4^{1}/_2$ hrs	60
14	Altdorf (Brüsti)-Engelberg	3	7 hrs	61
15	Altdorf (Brüsti)-Waldnacht-Attinghausen	3	6 hrs	63
16	Altdorf-Amsteg	1	$3^{1}/_2$ hrs	65
17	Amsteg-Gurtnellen-Göschenen	1-2	$5^{1}/_2$ hrs	65
18	Göschenen-St Gotthard Pass-Airolo	2-3	$7-7^{1}/_2$ hrs	66
19	Isenthal-Bauen	1	$1^{1}/_2$ -2 hrs	67
20	Isenthal-Furggelen-Scheidegg-Isenthal	2	$3^{1}/_2$ hrs	68
21	Isenthal-Sassigrat-St Jakob-Isenthal	3	$5-5^{1}/_2$ hrs	68
22	Isenthal-Sinsgauer Schonegg-Oberrickenbach	3	$6-6^{1}/_2$ hrs	69
23	Seelisberg-Niderbauen-Chulm	2-3	$3^{1}/_2$ hrs	71
24	Seelisberg-Hoch Flue-Sunnwil-Treib	2	$4^{1}/_2$ hrs	72
25	Pilatus Kulm-Ämsigen-Alpnachstad	2	3 hrs	74
26	Pilatus Kulm-Tomlishorn-Feldalp-Wängen	3	$3^{1}/_2$ hrs	75
27	Alpnachstad-Ämsigen-Pilatus Kulm	2-3	$4-4^{1}/_2$ hrs	76
28	Alpnachstad-Lütoldsmatt-Pilatus Kulm	2	5 hrs	76
29	Schwarzenbach-Milchbüelen-Schwarzenbach	2	$4^{1}/_2$ hrs	84
30	Bisistal-Balmer Grätli-Sahli	3	5 hrs	86
31	Bisistal (Sahli)-Firner Loch-Urnerboden	3	$4-4^{1}/_2$ hrs	88
32	Bisistal (Sahli)-Glattalp Hut	3	2 hrs	89
33	Glattalp Hut-Furggele	3	$2-2^{1}/_2$ hrs	91
34	Hinterthal-Liplisbüel	1-2	2 hrs	94
35	Liplisbüel-Seenalper Seeli	2-3	2 hrs	94
36	Liplisbüel-Chinzig Chulm-Alp Chinzertal-Liplisbüel	3	$6-6^{1}/_2$ hrs	95
37	Liplisbüel-Chinzig Chulm-Biel	3	$4^{1}/_2$ -5 hrs	97
38	Liplisbüel-Chinzig Chulm-Ratzi	3	$4^{1}/_2$ -5 hrs	98
39	Fruttli-Bergen Alp-Pragel Pass	1	$1^{1}/_2$ hrs	99
40	Klausenpass-Heidmanegg-Eggberge-Altdorf	2-3	9 hrs	108
41	Klausenpass-Äsch-Unterschächen	2	$2^{1}/_2$ -3 hrs	109
42	Unterschächen-Niralp-Brunnialp-Unterschächen	3	$6^{1}/_2$ -7 hrs	111
43	Unterschächen-Brunnialp-Sittlisalp-Unterschächen	2-3	$4^{1}/_2$ -5 hrs	113
44	Unterschachen-Stich Fülen-Erstfeld	3	9 hrs	115
45	Urnerboden-Zingel-Point 1778.9m	3	$1^{1}/_2$ hrs	119
46	Urnerboden-Zingel-Läcki	3	$1^{1}/_2$ hrs	120
47	Urnerboden-Firner Loch-Bisistal	3	5 hrs	121
48	Urnerboden-Braunwald	2-3	3 hrs	122
49	Urnerboden (Klus)-Gemsfairenhüttli	1	1 hr	123
50	Urnerboden-Klausenpass-Unterschächen	2-3	$4^{1}/_2$ hrs	124
51	Golzern-Golzerensee-Golzern	2	$1^{1}/_2$ hrs	130

Route		Grade	Time	Page
52	Golzern-Windgällen Hut	3	2 hrs	131
53	Golzern-Alp Stafel-Tritt-Maderanertal	3	5¹/₂ hrs	132
54	Bristen-Balmenschächen-Hüfi Hut	3	5¹/₂ hrs	134
55	Realp (Tiefenbach)-Albert Heim Hut	2	1-1¹/₂ hrs	141
56	Realp (Tiefenbach)-Blauseeli-Andermatt	3	5¹/₂ hrs	141
57	Realp-Oberstafel-Rotondo Hut	2-3	3¹/₂ hrs	142
58	Oberalp Pass-Fellilücke-Tresch Hut-Gurtnellen	3	6-6¹/₂ hrs	145
59	Oberalp Pass-Fellilücke-Lutersee-Andermatt	3	4¹/₂ hrs	148
60	Oberalp Pass-Lai da Tuma	2	1¹/₂ hrs	149
61	Göschenen-Gwüest-Göscheneralpsee	2	2¹/₂ -3 hrs	154
62	Göscheneralpsee-Vorder Röti-Point 1986m-Göscheneralpsee	2	3 hrs	155
63	Göscheneralpsee-Bergsee Hut	3	1¹/₂ -2 hrs	156
64	Bergsee Hut-Chelenalp Hut	3	3-3¹/₂ hrs	150
65	Göscheneralpsee-Chelenalp Hut	3	3¹/₂ hrs	158
66	Göscheneralpsee-Damma Hut	3	3 hrs	159
67	Damma Hut-Chelenalp Hut	3	3 hrs	160
68	Göschenertal (Voralp)-Voralp Hut	2	2¹/₂ hrs	160
69	Göschenen-Abfrutt-Salbit Hut	3	3 hrs	162
70	Wassen-Färnigen-Guferplatten	1-2	4 hrs	167
71	Meiental (Chli Sustli)-Sustli Hut	3	1 hr	168
72	Wassen-Färnigen-Sustli Hut	2-3	5 hrs	169
73	Wassen-Färnigen-Sewen Hut	3	4¹/₂ -5 hrs	169
74	Brünig Pass-Pilatus Kulm	3	4-5 days	175
75	Sarnen-Wichelsee-Alpnach	1	1 hr 45 mins	176
76	Melchsee Frutt-Tannenalp-Engstlensee	2	2 hrs	178
77	Melchsee Frutt-Jochpass-Engelberg	3	6-6¹/₂ hrs	179
78	Melchsee Frutt-Melchtal-Sachseln	2	4¹/₂ -5 hrs	181
79	Engelberg-Surenen Pass-Attinghausen	3	9-9¹/₂ hrs	187
80	Engelberg (Fürenalp)-Blackenalp-Engelberg	2	4¹/₂ -5 hrs	188
81	Engelberg (Fürenalp)-Ober Zieblen-Engelberg	2-3	2-2¹/₂ hrs	190
82	Engelberg-Ober Zieblen-Dagenstal-Engelberg	3	5¹/₂ hrs	191
83	Engelberg-Fürenalp-Stauber-Engelberg	3	7¹/₂ -8 hrs	193
84	Engelberg-Stäfeli-Spannort Hut	3	4 hrs	194
85	Engelberg-Trübsee-Unter Trübsee-Engelberg	2-3	4-4¹/₂ hrs	194
86	Engelberg-Jochpass-Engstlenalp	3	4¹/₂ -5 hrs	196
87	Engelberg-Juchli Pass-Melchtal	3	6¹/₂ -7 hrs	197
88	Engelberg (Brunni)-Brunni Hut	2-3	40 mins	198
89	Engelberg (Brunni)-Rugghubel Hut	3	2¹/₂ -3 hrs	198
90	Engelberg (Brunni)-Oberrickenbach-Niederrickenbach	3	6-6¹/₂ hrs	199

Printed by CARNMOR PRINT & DESIGN, 95-97 LONDON ROAD, PRESTON, LANCASHIRE, UK.

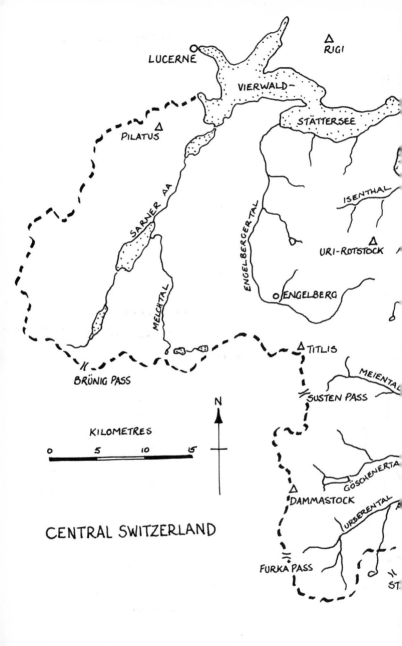

CENTRAL SWITZERLAND